STAND UP TO ELDER FINANCIAL ABU$E

JOHN ROTONDI, CFE, CPA

CONTENTS

CONTENTS

PREFACE

In his poem, *Beautiful Old Age*, D.H. Lawrence wrote, "It ought to be lovely to be old." However, "lovely" is not how many aged men and women feel after being swindled. While those 65 and older comprise about an eighth of the U.S. population, they represent about a third of scam victims, according to Sid Kirchheimer of the American Association of Retired Persons (AARP). Not one day goes by without a news story about a despicable financial act committed against someone who is elderly. The abuser not only takes the victim's money, but the victim's trust in society that they've built up over the years; their independence in taking care of themselves, including their financial needs; and their pride in making sound judgments. After the crime, these casualties are left emotionally, physically, and financially drained. We are well past the time that says, "Enough is enough." More than any other age group, those 65 or older are falling victim to frauds because they are often easily accessible and socially isolated as they reach their retirement years, spending more time at home. Also, they experience declining physical and mental well-being as they grow older, causing the fraudster to take advantage of their decreased cognitive abilities. Finally, and most importantly, significant assets are controlled by retirees, who have accumulated them over a lifetime of hard work. Con artists go where the money is, and it's with seniors. Older Americans control trillions of dollars of wealth, a figure that makes scammers salivate. Have you ever succumbed to a fraudster's deception, or know someone who has? If so, this is the book for you.

Don't ever say to yourself, "This can't possibly happen to me." It can, and, for some of you, it has, but you may not even know it. Realize that it's not your fault. You did nothing wrong, so don't blame yourself. None of us is too smart for someone as cunning as a determined financial scammer. Start protecting yourself, and your money, from these charlatans. We'll get into the fraudster's mind to understand their motivations and tricks of the trade, and your mind, so you can understand your own vulnerabilities to these tactics. We'll go through some of the financial scams that are targeted towards the elderly, along with recommendations for the victims, and their loved ones, to follow. Investigators and regulators who care about these sages of wisdom, and want to protect them from the dregs of society, will also learn from the scenarios presented herein, and will be better prepared to follow-up on suspicious activity that might indicate a senior has been financially abused. And, finally, lawmakers will learn of the extent of the problem, and the gaps in our laws that need to be closed, if seniors are to be better protected. This book is for all fraud fighters – victims, family and friends, caretakers, lawmakers, investigators, and regulators, anyone who cares about the scourge of elder financial abuse, and wants to do something to combat it. We must work together to get it done. As Edmund Burke, the Irish statesman was reported to have said, "The only thing necessary for the triumph of evil is for good men to do nothing." When it comes to protecting ourselves from street criminals, we turn on our outdoor lights, lock our doors, get an alarm system, put our valuables in a safe, tell our neighbors to pick up our mail and newspapers when we are away, but what do we do to protect ourselves from the sophisticated and slick fraudster? When it comes to the innovative, less violent, financial crimes, we do little. These, and the people who commit them, need to be stopped, and this book will empower you to do just that. So, let's get started on the journey to doing something.

Port Washington, New York

April 30, 2017

PART I
The Problem

CHAPTER 1
Do the Right Thing

Elder financial abuse has been, and continues to be, a growing problem. According to *Fraud*, a book written by Professor Edward J. Balleisen, the considerable growth in the elder population by the 1960s encouraged scams targeting seniors. Since then, those aged 65 and older, along with their wealth, have only continued to grow exponentially. According to the Administration on Aging (AoA), an agency of the U.S. Department of Health and Human Services, there were 46.2 million Americans who were 65 years or older in 2014 (the latest year for which data is available). This is expected to be about 98 million in 2060. In the meantime, seniors hold tens of trillions of dollars of wealth, ready to be transferred to the next generation, or to charities, as they desire, while the scammer eyes this figure, as well as opportunity, and drools. As the economy has grown, so have frauds. Tackling elder financial abuse will only make the economy more efficient, as financial resources go to their intended domestic targets, instead of overseas swindlers. Fraud is every American's loss, and, therefore, every American's problem.

What is elder abuse? Before I get to elder financial abuse, let me briefly discuss elder abuse in general. According to the Social Security Act, elder abuse is an intentional or negligent act by someone that causes harm to anyone that is 60 years of age or older. Sometimes the harm is physical. Sometimes it's psychological. Sometimes it's financial. And sometimes it's all three at once. Elder abuse is becoming more of a problem as the population ages. In the U.S., about 10,000 people turn 65 each day, a pattern that is expected to continue for the next 15 years, according to the Pew Research Center.

What do we know about elder abuse? Most often, elder abuse comes to our attention through media headlines about celebrities or other famous people who have been abused. Take the late actor, Mickey Rooney, whose Hollywood career spanned almost nine decades, during which he appeared in such well known movies as *Babes in Arms* and *The Human Comedy*. But by the time Rooney celebrated his 90th birthday in September 2010, with Donald Trump, incidentally, and other famous Hollywood personalities of The Mickster's heyday, the abuse he had been experiencing was no laughing matter. The actor eventually brought a case against two of his stepchildren for financial, as well as physical, abuse. He was an advocate for senior rights and testified in Congress. His powerful testimony gives insight into what is going on inside the mind of an elder abuse victim. Here are some brief snippets of his testimony from March 2, 2011 to the Special Committee on Aging of the U.S. Senate:

"When it happens, you feel scared, disappointed – yes, and angry. And you can't believe that it's happening to you. You feel overwhelmed. The strength you need to fight it. Complicated. You're afraid, but you're also thinking about your other family members, about the potential criticism of your family, your friends. People you know, they may not want to accept the dysfunction that you feel and need to share...."

"You can be in control of your life one minute, ladies and gentlemen, and in the next minute, like that, you have absolutely, believe it or not, no control of your life. Sometimes this happens quickly, but other times it's very, very gradual. You might wonder when all this truly began."

"In my case, I was eventually and completely stripped of the ability to make even the most basic decisions – where we go or what do we do – decisions that everyone likes to make."

"I felt trapped, scared, used, and frustrated. And, above all, when a man feels helpless, it's terrible. And I was helpless."

"For years, I suffered silently. I didn't want to tell anybody. I couldn't muster the courage. And you have to have courage to say – 'I need help.' And I knew I needed it."

It's most important that family members and friends treat seniors who have been abused as victims, because that's what they are – victims, and they need our support. Give them understanding, kindness, love, and respect. Don't blame them for what happened – for the loss of money, or whatever else might have befallen them.

Oftentimes in these instances, there's collateral damage. It turns out that Kelly Rooney, The Mickster's daughter, was a victim as well. During her father's legal battle she was unable to visit him, so now she is fighting for a state bill in Nebraska that would prevent the elderly from being isolated from their family members, according to the *Omaha World-Herald*. Unlike some Congressional bills, which can seem as long, and feel as dense, as a college textbook, this state bill is less than two pages. The intent of the legislation, which was introduced by Democratic State Senator Patty Pansing Brooks, is to "allow family members to remain connected" to their loved ones and, in so doing, prohibits a senior's caregiver, which can be another family member or not, from arbitrarily denying visitation rights to a family member. If a family member is not being allowed a visit, then they may petition the district court in order to obtain their right to do so. The court process would be sped up if the elderly person's health is deteriorating. And, if the caregiver is intentionally isolating the elderly person from being visited, then they may be required to pay the court costs, as well as reasonable attorney's fees of the family member bringing the case. Of course, if the senior is of sound mind, then they have the discretion to not allow visits of any particular person.

Since I've touched on Hollywood, two films that concern elder abuse that I recommend you watch, particularly if you're interested in this topic are *Amour* and *Nebraska*, from 2012 and 2013, respectively. *Amour* (Love) is a French-language drama about a married octogenarian couple – Georges and Ann, both retired music teachers. *Nebraska* is a dark comedy about an aging father who takes a trip, accompanied by his son, from his home in Montana to Nebraska in order to claim a million-dollar sweepstakes prize. For a look at the financial exploitation of the elderly, I'd recommend the 2013 Emmy-award winning documentary entitled, *Fleeced: Speaking Out Against Senior Financial Abuse*, which reports on both legal and illegal businesses that prey on seniors, and the real-life impact it has on them and their families. It shows the transformation of seniors from abuse victims, losing their hard-earned money, to committed advocates, speaking out to affect change and help prevent financial exploitation.

Let's discuss another case, that of Harper Lee, who is the author of the Pulitzer Prize-winning *To Kill a Mockingbird* and *Go Set a Watchman*. In 2013, at age 87, Lee, now deceased, filed a lawsuit against her former literary agent, alleging that he had taken advantage of her physical state in order to gain control of her royalty payments. No sooner was this case settled, than controversy about her mental state in her agreeing to the publication of *Go Set a Watchman* came to the fore. The Alabama Securities Commission, on behalf of the Alabama Human Resources Department, investigated the allegations, made anonymously by a doctor in her community, and ultimately found no evidence of financial fraud. According to *The Birmingham News*, a lawyer with the Alabama Securities Commission, stated at the time: "We traveled to the nursing home to talk to Ms. Lee at the request of the Alabama Department of Human Resources. We have since closed our files on the matter." This case demonstrates that oftentimes, allegations of mistreatment of the elderly are complicated and may not be resolved to everyone's satisfaction. The important lessons are to say something, even anonymously, if you see something, so kudos to the doctor that reported it. Credit should also be given to the Alabama authorities for taking it seriously enough to investigate. One only hopes that Lee was represented by these officials as thoroughly and honorably as Atticus Finch represented Tom Robinson.

I believe the Brooke Astor case is the one we are most familiar with, as many of us are devout *Page Six* followers. For those who are not, Astor, who lived to 105, was the socialite of all socialites. More than that, believing that wealth "is like manure; it's not worth a thing unless it's spread around," as reported by *The New York Times*, she devoted her life to giving it away through her philanthropic endeavors, which intensified as she aged and culminated in her being awarded the Presidential Medal of Freedom in 1998. This great American philanthropist, who lived young at heart, was abused, both financially and physically, by her only son – Anthony Marshall. Incidentally, she was also physically abused by her first husband – John Dryden Kuser, who was Anthony's father. It was Marshall's son, Philip, who originally brought the abuse charges against his father. About reporting his father's abuse toward his grandmother, Philip said, "As weird as it is, you have to do the right thing," according to the *New York Daily News*. Marshall, after being convicted of grand larceny, was sentenced to 1-3 years in prison, but only served 8 weeks after being granted parole because of his frail and deteriorating health.

Lessons Learned

So, I believe all of these cases offer us some important lessons:

If it happened to them, then it can happen to any of us. Abuse is not discriminating. It can happen to the famous, and the not-so-famous. It can happen to the rich, the middle class, and the poor. It can happen to your family, your friend, and your neighbor. It can happen to you.

If you are a senior and you're being abused reach out for help now. There are many agencies that are there to help you, no matter what abuse you are suffering. The Resources section of this book has the names and contact information of those assigned to help you.

Speak up for your family member, friend, and neighbor who is being abused. When they have no voice, you must be their voice. The Resources section of this book has the names and contact information of those assigned to help them.

Start end-of-life and estate planning while you are physically and mentally healthy. Benjamin Franklin called death one of the two things (taxes being the other) that are certain. Since it's sure to happen, we might as well be prepared before it does.

What is the extent of the elder abuse problem? According to the National Council on Aging (https://www.ncoa.org), which is an organization that is designed to help those 60 and over meet the challenges of aging by provide community programs and services, online help, and advocacy in partnership with nonprofit organizations, government, and businesses, these are the grim statistics: at least 1 in 9 Americans over age 60 has experienced elder abuse; as many as 5 million seniors are abused each year; about 90% of elder abuse is committed by a family member; women and the very old are most likely to be abused; and 21% of the allegations of mistreatment concern elder financial abuse.

The National Elder Mistreatment Study, which was funded by the U.S. Department of Justice, noted that about 4.6% of adults over age 60 reported experiencing some form of emotional mistreatment in the past year, and only 8% of these individuals reported the event to the police. Thus, emotional mistreatment, although common, is rarely reported, and even less frequently acted upon, by criminal justice authorities. According to the study, emotional mistreatment is "legal" and, though cruel, lacks any criminal justice system remedy, virtually assuring its sustained frequency. The prevalence of elder physical mistreatment was lower, at 1.6%. Potential neglect, which the study defined "as instances where an older adult identified a specific essential need that was not being met; but did not necessarily indicate that anyone had been designated to meet that need" had been reported by 5.1% of study respondents. According to the study, the prevalence of financial exploitation by family members in one form or another in the recent past was noted in over 5% of respondents, making this abuse by trusted individuals, extremely high and common. Because of this, the study recommended that dedicated resources and civil remedies be directed toward this type of mistreatment (e.g., prosecutors assigned to handling financial abuse cases in geographic regions with high numbers of older adults).

How does the world commemorate the scourge of elder abuse? Each year, on June 15th, the United Nations commemorates World Elder Abuse Awareness Day.

CHAPTER 2
The Signature Crime of the 21st Century

What is elder financial abuse? Elder financial abuse is generally defined as the improper or unlawful use of a senior's funds, property, or other assets. Here are some examples: (1) taking a senior's property, including money, directly or indirectly, by means of fraud or deception. Most of the scams discussed later concern a criminal's indirect means of obtaining the money by, for instance, having the senior make a wire transfer to him because the senior believed his lies; (2) using a senior's property without permission; (3) offering to buy a senior's property, whether personal property or real estate, but not paying what it's really worth; (4) forging their signature on checks or other documents; (5) pressuring a senior into signing a will, durable power of attorney, contract, or other legal document that they don't understand, don't really want to sign, or are not in a condition to sign because, for instance, they are suffering from dementia; (6) using a senior's credit, debit, or automated teller machine (ATM) card; (7) promising lifelong care in exchange for money or property and then not delivering it; and (8) selling investments to seniors that lack full disclosures, aren't in their best interests, or are outright frauds.

In the Brooke Astor case, Anthony Marshall's lawyer, who conspired with Marshall against Astor, was convicted of forging her signature on her will. And they were both convicted of forcing her to sign a codicil (an amendment to her will) when she was incompetent to do so, according to the *New York Post*.

What is the cost of elder financial abuse? The estimated annual loss to victims of elder financial abuse, which has been called "a hidden epidemic and the signature crime of the 21st Century" by Hubert H. "Skip" Humphrey III of the Consumer Financial Protection Bureau (CFPB), is $2.9 billion, according to one estimate issued by MetLife. A more recent study, released by True Link, estimates that 36.9% of seniors are affected by financial abuse in any five-year period. They put the cost of elder financial abuse at $36.48 billion annually, broken down as follows: $16.99 billion is lost to *financial exploitation*, which they define as "the use of misleading or confusing language – often combined with social pressure and tactics that take advantage of cognitive decline and memory loss – to obtain a senior's consent to take his or her money;" $12.76 billion is lost to *criminal fraud*, which is "explicitly illegal activity, such as the grandparent scam, the Nigerian prince scam, or identity theft and credit card fraud;" and $6.67 billion is lost to *caregiver abuse*, which is "deceit or theft enabled by a trusting relationship – typically a family member but sometimes a paid helper, friend, lawyer, accountant, or financial manager." Because a lot goes unreported, it is likely higher. The emotional toll, which cannot be measured in dollars and cents, is far worse. It destroys peoples' lives.

Why are the elderly targeted? There are many reasons that the elderly are targeted. These are some of them: (1) seniors have more savings and disposable income because of a lifetime of hard work; (2) many live alone, so won't have the opportunity to consult with others, and many spend a lot of time at home, which makes them more available for bogus telemarketing calls or other solicitations; (3) seniors are more trusting, polite, and don't like to say "No," so the scammer is easily able to develop a rapport and trust relationship with the victim that ultimately leads to the victim being manipulated; (4) some may suffer from cognitive impairment, such as Alzheimer's disease; and (5) they are less likely to report the incident because they don't want to damage their pride or lose their independence. Additionally, they may seek to avoid embarrassment, ridicule, or giving their colleagues and acquaintances the benefit of enjoying their damaged financial predicament.

Why would someone want to scam the elderly? Any financial crime, including financial crimes against the elderly, can be thought of as culminating from the *Fraud Triangle* paradigm, which is a three-sided framework, consisting of *Incentive/Pressure*, *Opportunity*, and *Rationalization*, for explaining why criminals take depraved actions against the elderly. First, there is *Incentive/Pressure* that causes the criminal to initiate his act. It can be money problems, the desire to live a certain lifestyle, or the need to please someone. For Anthony Marshall, Brooke Astor's son, it was likely the latter two. Even though he was already quite wealthy, grandees in these circles are always looking for more. The wealth they already have is not enough, when compared to others in the social-climbing upper-crust. Also, his wife appeared to be putting pressure on him to act as he did, according to his son Philip, who referred to her as a "sugar-coated poison pill," according to the *New York Daily News*. Next, there is *Opportunity*. This is the circumstance that allows a criminal act to occur. While Marshall took advantage of his mother's physical condition, he also, with his attorney, conspired to re-write his mother's intentions, as expressed in her will, in effect creating his own opportunities. Such opportunities occur because of a breakdown in controls. There is no greater control, in the realm of elder financial abuse, than a senior's own sharp faculties. So, when these start to wither away, so does the control, which only enhances the opportunity to commit the criminal act. Finally, there is *Rationalization*, which is the reasoning and justification in the criminal's mind that what he did was not wrong, and that he deserved the gains that came to him. Marshall never testified at his trial, so we don't know what explanation he may have provided. He may have felt entitled to her wealth because he was Astor's only child and she was aging. In his mind, he may have thought that the money should naturally go to him. According to his lawyers, Marshall was legally entitled to give himself gifts from his mother's fortune and he was confident that she wanted him to have them, according to the *Daily Mail*.

The *Fraud Triangle* helps us begin to better understand the criminal mind. A family member that steals from an elderly parent or other elderly relative may not think of it as stealing. They may rationalize what they are doing, particularly if they are, to some extent, taking care of the individual.

What types of methods do criminals use to scam seniors? Scammers ask a lot of questions in order to get to know the victim. They use this information to tailor their pitch. These are some of the methods in the fraudster's toolbox: With *Friendship*, the scammer develops a rapport and builds trust with the victim. With *Authority*, the scammer may claim he is from the "Social Security Administration," "Microsoft Tech Support," or the "Police." With *Scarcity*, the scammer may say, "You must act now before the opportunity is gone." With *Reciprocity*, the scammer may represent to you that his company will pick up certain fees that are required to receive lottery winnings. Then he says that you just need to pick up the remaining fees. With *Consensus*, the scammer may claim others have won this lottery or made this investment. Because these time-tested methods are very effective, and tailored to the potential victim, anyone can be scammed. I'll discuss these methods in more depth later on.

What schemes should I beware of? There are many schemes that you should beware of, and they are only limited by the depth of a fraudster's cunning.

Beware of calls promising prizes, gifts, or grants. The most dangerous word from any caller could be, "Congratulations!" If you receive any telephone call from anyone about something you've won – like a vacation, or are entitled to – like a government grant, and the caller starts asking you for personal information, particularly sensitive information like social security or credit card or bank account numbers, don't provide it. They are looking for something in return. In order for you to get your prize, they tell you, you have to pay a small fee.

But, sometimes they don't mention the fee. They just take it from you, without you suspecting it, once you provide your bank account number for the purpose of them allegedly wiring you the money they say you're entitled to. If any money is moved, it'll be from your bank account to the fraudster's bank account. Alternatively, you may be inclined to do as they ask and drive to your local Walgreens to buy an Amazon gift card, scratch off the metallic-looking substance to get the claim code, and then provide it to them. Providing the code will give them control of the card, which they can use for themselves or sell to another party. Don't play this "I'll scratch your back, if you scratch mine" game. Never put up money, or personal information, to get money.

Below is an excerpt of a call, from the 202 area code (Washington, DC), or so it seemed, that I recently received from a scammer, using the fictitious name "Roger Miller," and posing as a U.S. government employee:

Roger Miller *[in a heavy South Asian accent] Hello. This is Mr. John Rotondi?*

Me *Yes. This is John Rotondi.*

Roger Miller *This is Roger Miller calling from the United States Federal Grant Department.*

Me *The U.S. Federal Grant Department? I must have missed that in Government 101. How can I help you?*

Roger Miller *We did a survey. Because you are a good citizen, pay your bills on time, and pay your taxes, you have been selected by the federal government for a loyalty grant. Nine hundred people have been selected and you, Mr. John, are one of them. This grant is $14,566. Would you like your money today?*

Me *Yes. That's great news. Where are you calling from?*

Roger Miller *(a long pause, as he refers to his script) I'm calling from Washington, DC.*

Me *How is the weather down in DC?*

Roger Miller *(a longer pause) Mr. John, do you want your money or not?*

Me *Well, it's not my money yet. I was just wondering what the temperature is in DC. Do you know?*

Roger Miller *(pause) We don't know as we're inside all day.*

Me *It's 2:30 in the afternoon. You haven't had a chance to get out for lunch yet?*

Roger Miller F_____you, Mr. John!

I was able to elicit from the scammer the ill-will and nastiness that is at the heart of their character. They don't care about you, they're only looking to separate you from your money. Now I don't recommend that you engage the scammer. The best advice I can give you is to just hang up on the caller, without any need to be polite. As the above call demonstrates, they're only courteous as long as you're fully cooperative, and subservient, with them. It's when they see your take-charge attitude that you'll see them expose their true selves. If the call continued, "Roger" would have asked me to verify some information, such as my address and email, which he already had. Scammers purchase contact lists, just as other telemarketing firms do. Having this information makes them seem legitimate, when we know they're not. If I sounded like I was ready to pay, he would then hand me off to a "closer" who would call me in a few minutes. In order to wire the proceeds to me, the closer would have eventually asked for my bank's name, bank account number, and bank debit card number with the accompanying "CVV code" (an anti-fraud security feature). If I didn't have any of those, he would have asked that I drive, with him still on the smartphone line, to a well-known local retailer where I could purchase an iTunes or Amazon gift card, and he'd ask me to load it with upwards of $600 dollars. Then he'd ask me for the claim code, and my $600 would be gone.

This fraud – the "government grant scam" – has been going on for years, although with various iterations. It may have become more popular recently because of a change in the U.S. presidential administration. With such a change, there are revisions to policies and laws, so the scammers, who follow the news closely, believe someone out there might just fall for it, and they, unfortunately, do. The Federal Trade Commission (FTC), a *real* government agency that promotes consumer protection, issued a press release on the "government grant scam" in September 2006.

Another common scam involves "unclaimed property." There are several variations of this. You may receive in the mail a "Notice of Unclaimed Property." What you haven't claimed is silver or gold coins that are going to cost you more than they are worth. (Come to think of it, there are lots of things I haven't "claimed." Of course, they mean "bought.") Take a pass. Another, more sinister, variation, is a scammer claiming that you have "unclaimed property" with a particular state, say Texas, and in order for them to retrieve it for you, you need to pay a fee. They collect the fee from you, but it's unlikely you'll hear from them again.

Find, and claim, any money that may be owed to you, for free. There are billions of dollars sitting in government, or other organization, coffers waiting to be claimed by someone entitled to it. Maybe, that's you or a family member. "So, how do I get my hands on this?" you ask. Read on.

Unclaimed Property (From U.S. States)

State governments are holding upwards of $50 billion in unclaimed property. Under state escheatment laws, any financial assets that you, or your relatives, have revert back to the state if they are considered abandoned. Unclaimed property is based on laws in every state that calls for such property to revert back to the state general fund after a certain period of time. The term "escheat" derives from the Latin ex-cadere and means "to fall out." Essentially, it's a process wherein your assets fall out from under your control to the state's control. All states require businesses to report to them when personal property has been abandoned after a period of time specified by law – often five years. Before the assets can be considered unclaimed, the business must make a diligent effort to try to locate the owner. If the business is unable to do so, and the account (if applicable) has remained inactive for the requisite period, the business must report the account to the state where it's held. The state then claims the account through a process called "escheatment." If any of your assets (e.g., bank or other financial account, unpaid wages, utility deposit) have been escheated to the state you don't need to pay anyone to retrieve them. You can determine on your own if you are owed money by going to a certain websites. One is https://www.missingmoney.com, where you'll be asked to enter you first and last name and current state of residence. A search will be done of all states. Other experts recommend using https://www.unclaimed.org/. With this website, you'll have to go state by state (it also includes Canadian Provinces and U.S. territories), but you'll tend to get better results. When searching, keep in mind that your name may have been incorrectly spelled or entered when held at the applicable institution, so you may want to try various spellings and rearrangements of your first and last name. You may be able to get variations of your name from your credit report, which can be obtained free, as I'll show in the Resources section of this book. A common error is the omission of the last letter of your last name, so try omitting that when searching. Also, try entering your last name as your first, and your first name as your last. Good luck! If you're successful, you can then determine a particular state's requirements when claiming money by going to that state's website through https://www.unclaimed.org/. If you believe you have unclaimed property, the state will require you to complete a claim form and send them information about yourself to verify your ownership of the unclaimed property.

Unclaimed Life Insurance Proceeds

Regulators, in recent years, have gone after life insurers for selectively using the Social Security Death Index (SSDI), which is free and can be accessed here: http://search.ancestry.com/search/db.aspx?dbid=3693. Life insurers were alleged to be using the SSDI in order to stop payments to annuity holders who had died, but not using it to pay beneficiaries of life insurance policies. For life insurance benefits that aren't held by the state yet, through the escheatment process, you can try checking the insurer's website directly. For example, MetLife has a search function here: https://www.metlife.com/policyfinder/index.html. Alternatively, the National Association of Insurance Commissioners (NAIC) provides a Life Insurance Policy Locator Service that helps you locate the life insurance policies and annuity contracts of a deceased family member. You can access it here: https://eapps.naic.org/life-policy-locator/#/welcome. The NAIC, in turn, will send your request to participating life insurance and annuity companies and will ask them to search their records to determine whether they have an individual life insurance policy or annuity contract in the name of the deceased. It may take up to ninety business days to be contacted. Contact your state's insurance department if you have any issues with a particular insurer.

Unclaimed Retirement Benefits

According to the Pension Benefit Guaranty Corporation

(PBGC), there are more than 38,000 people who haven't claimed over $300 million in pension benefits they are owed. The PBGC is a U.S. government agency created by the Employee Retirement Income Security Act (ERISA) of 1974 to protect pension benefits in private-sector defined benefit plans, which pay a set monthly amount at retirement. If your pension plan ends without sufficient money to pay all benefits, PBGC's insurance program will pay you the benefit provided by your pension plan up to the limits set by law. Most people, however, receive the full benefit they had earned before the plan ended. The states with the most missing pension participants and money to be claimed are: New York (7,031/$42.38 million), Illinois (4,129/$79.63 million), California (3,082/$8.52 million), Texas (2,487/$12.32 million), New Jersey (2,288/$12.84 million), and Ohio (2,109/$15.22 million).

You may have unclaimed retirement benefits waiting for you. Go to this link to find out: https://search.pbgc.gov/search/MP/Mp?col=nc&filter=c&tab=mp. For employer sponsored retirement plans, such as defined contribution plans, i.e., 401(k), or profit sharing plans, you can search the database of the National Registry of Unclaimed Retirement Benefits, which is located here: https://www.unclaimedretirementbenefits.com/SSNSearch.aspx

Undeliverable U.S. Government Savings Notes and Bonds
According to the U.S. Treasury Department, each year, over 15,000 savings bonds and 25,000 interest payments are returned to them as undeliverable. In addition, as of December 31, 2016, over 58 million savings bonds (Series A, B, C, D, E, EE, F, G, H, HH, J, and K), as well as savings notes, worth over $23 billion, have stopped earning interest, but haven't been cashed. "Treasury Hunt," a search tool, tells you about savings bonds no longer earning interest. If these bonds or notes belong to you, you'll want to reinvest them so your money can start

working for you again. Use the "Start Search" button at this website: https://www.treasuryhunt.gov. Although "Treasury Hunt" is updated monthly, it's a limited database in that it doesn't contain a record of all savings notes and bonds.

Undeliverable Federal Tax Refunds

Over the last few years, the Internal Revenue Service (IRS) has announced that it was unable to deliver tax refunds, amounting to between $100-200 million to tens of thousands of taxpayers. For example, In November 2011 the IRS said it was looking to return $153.3 million to 99,123 taxpayers. However, the tax refund checks could not be delivered because of mailing address errors. Undelivered refund checks average $1,547 that year. Click on the "Where's My Refund?" button at https://www.irs.gov/refunds to see if you are due a refund, but haven't received it. Call the IRS if it has been twenty-one days or more since you filed your return electronically, more than six weeks since you mailed your paper return, or the "Where's My Refund?" tool directs you to contact them.

Beware of emails promising a gift card. The most dangerous words from any email may be "Thank you." These emails may look like they come from Walgreens or Amazon, or some other well-known, brand name online or bricks and mortar retailer. The giveaway that it's a scam is typically the unusual email address that it comes from. Don't click on any boxes or links, so as to avoid falling into the scammer's trap. Their intent is to get their grimy hands on your personal information. Mark it as spam, and delete it.

What can I do to stop the endless calls I receive from these scammers? In order to avoid incessant calls, be stringy with your personal information, even when the caller is asking for just your name, email address, and phone number. If you tend to participate in even legitimate sweepstakes or coin purchase deals, then you'll be put on a list, and that list will be sold to not only telemarketers, but to scammers looking for a sucker. And, then, the calls to you are going to start popping up like mushrooms from Umbria, Italy in late spring.

What can I do to help fight scams? Report any scam you experience to a governmental consumer protection agency. For example, it can be reported with as much detail as you're comfortable with, to the Federal Trade Commission. FTC complaints can be reported here: https://www.ftccomplaintassistant.gov/#&panel1-1 Small frauds turn into big ones, so report them. Scammers are known to parlay the money they've made in seemingly insignificant rackets into major scams, so stop them dead in their tracks. If you don't report it, then the fraudster got you again. Once when he took your money and the second time when he counted on you not reporting it.

Is there anything else that I should be thinking about now, before I get older and my memory starts to fade? Consider establishing a *will, living trust, durable power of attorney, health care proxy,* and *living will.* A *will* or *testament* is a legal document by which you, the testator, name someone to manage your estate and provide for the distribution of your property at death. A *living trust* is a legal document that allows you, or the person you name as trustee, to transfer ownership of your assets to a trust. While you have control over the assets during your life, the assets go to those you name once you die. It allows your heirs to avoid probate. A *durable power of attorney,* which lasts until you die or it is revoked, is a legal document that allows someone else to take over your financial matters if needed, i.e., if you become incapacitated. Choose someone responsible and reliable, someone who you trust to act in your best interest, keep accurate records, and avoid any conflicts of interest. A *health care proxy* or *health care power of attorney* is a legal document that allows a patient to appoint an agent to make health care decisions according to the patient's wishes, in the event that the primary individual is incapable of executing such decisions. A *living will* is a legal document that expresses your health care wishes when you cannot communicate them personally. It is not used to name a proxy – someone to act on your behalf. Once completed and executed, it should be provided to your doctor or others involved in your health care, close family members, and your attorney.

How can I protect myself from elder financial abuse?

Sun Tzu, the Chinese general and military strategist who penned the treatise *The Art of War*, wrote, "Every battle is won before it's even fought." Follow the gist of his quote. Prepare yourself now to combat elder financial abuse, by educating yourself about the various scams out there and how they work, by being skeptical and verifying what you are told, and by being patient and deliberate before forking-over your money or personal information. By following these steps, when you face the battle, whether that battle is a call from a lottery scammer, or a bogus can't-lose investment opportunity, or an email from a Nigerian prince promising you a piece of a vast fortune, you'll already have won because you'll know what to do and what not to do.

Protect yourself from scams by protecting your money and personal information. Never give money (whether cash, cashier's check, check, money order, wire transfer) or personal information (whether banking account number, credit card number, or social security number) or take instructions from anyone based on unsolicited contact – when they've contacted you.

Only give money or personal information when you have independently verified, and are certain of, the recipient's organization and purpose and they need the money or information for legitimate reasons. Even then, know the rules of the road. For instance, even when an organization or individual is legitimate, you generally don't want to give out your full social security number (SSN) when there's no rationale for them to have it. Take doctors, hospitals, and other health care providers, for example. Says *Consumer Reports* medical adviser, Orly Avitzur, MBA, MD, "There's really no reason to give your doctor or hospital your Social Security number. Insurers have your unique subscriber number and that's what we use to submit claims." Dr. Avitzur's medical office stopped asking patients for their numbers about five years ago. Those on Medicare, however, have no choice but to share their SSN with a health care provider, for now, because their Medicare ID is their SSN. However, the Medicare Access and CHIP Reauthorization Act (MACRA) of 2015 requires the Centers For Medicare and Medicaid Services (CMS), which is a federal agency within the U.S. Department of Health and Human Services (HHS) that administers Medicare, to remove SSNs from all Medicare cards by April 2019. A new Medicare Beneficiary Identifier (MBI) will replace the SSN. CMS will begin mailing the new cards with the unique MBI in April 2018. By the way, because of this change, it's expected that fraudster's will commence a new scam to get your personal information. They'll call you and tell you they're from "CMS" or "HHS" and will be sending out your new Medicare card, but before they do, they need to verify your information. "What's your Social Security Number?" they'll ask. Don't fall for it. Remember, they're calling you, and you don't give out information on unsolicited calls.

In the meantime, share your SSN with your health care providers (in the form of your Medicare card), so they can get paid by Medicare, on your first visit to the provider. After that visit make a copy of your original card, black out all but the last four digits of your SSN, make another copy of that copy, and carry that second copy with you to the doctor or hospital. Destroy the first copy because, if you look at the back of it, you may be able to make out the full SSN, and so may someone who is up to no good. Place your Medicare card in a safe place (not your purse or wallet). In this way, you won't have to carry your original card, with your complete SSN, at all times.

Your best protection is to educate yourself to recognize a scam and how to handle it. Never hesitate to contact your local police or other authorities. Reading this book, and using it as a reference guide, is your first step in educating yourself about scams. As some of the more common and egregious frauds are discussed in the proceeding chapters, there will be recommendations for the victim, as well as their family members and friends, to take.

PART II

Common Frauds

CHAPTER 3
A Losing Bet For Seniors and a Jackpot For Scammers

What is international lottery fraud? One particular form of financial abuse that is pulled off against the elderly that I'd like to discuss is international lottery fraud. International lottery fraud typically works in one of two ways. In one version, a victim may get an unsolicited phone call or email from someone notifying them that they've won a lottery or some other prize. In order to collect the winnings, however, they must first send a small sum of money to pay for processing fees or taxes. Victims immediately wire the money, but never get their "winnings." The result is that they're now out the money they paid for "fees" or "taxes." Alternatively, a victim may get an unsolicited check and letter notifying the recipient that they've won a lottery, and with instructions to deposit the check and immediately wire a portion of it back to cover processing fees or taxes. Again, the victims don't get their winnings. Soon after this, the victim learns that the check is counterfeit and has bounced, but they have already wired the money to cover the "fees" or "taxes" and can't get it back. And they're on the hook to pay their banks back for any money they withdrew.

U.S. Federal Trade Commission statistics show that complaints regarding "Prizes, Sweepstakes, and Lotteries" have increased from about 9,000 in 2001 to about 140,136 in 2015. Over the past six years it has been in the top five of their most reported complaints. It's become such a problem that the U.S. Postal Service has started a campaign to stop it. In fact, they sent out a large postcard that on its face read, "IF YOU HAVE TO SEND $250 TO CLAIM YOUR PRIZE ODDS ARE IT'S A SCAM YOU COULD LOSE," to all their postal customers in March 2013. (Apparently, times don't change that much, for in

25

1866 the postal service alerted their customers with a handbill they distributed that read, "TAKE WARNING! Beware of Jewelry and Lottery Swindlers!," according to Professor Balleisen's *Fraud*.)

Many of the unsolicited calls appear as a local number, if you have caller ID, but that doesn't mean the call is coming from a local area. Criminals know that you're more likely to pick up the phone when it appears as a local number, so they use technology to disguise the originating geographic area of their call. This is a method that is known as "phone spoofing." For instance, a criminal can purchase a magicJackTM, which is a device that deploys Voice over Internet Protocol (VoIP) technology, allowing the user to employ a telephone number from any area code and to make local and long-distance calls to the U.S. and Canada from anywhere they can secure an internet connection.

One such person that was targeted by these scammers is Norman Breidenbaugh, who is an 85-year old former U.S. Navy veteran from Baltimore, Maryland. When he received the solicitation about having won over $1 million, he thought it was a godsend because his wife was ill and he was worried he wouldn't have enough money to take care of her. The $1 million plus lottery prize would more than take care of her medical expenses, if it were real. What Mr. Breidenbaugh thought was a godsend turned into a financial and emotional catastrophe, as he managed to lose $400,000 to these scammers over a period of 6 years. His wife has since died and he has lost his house.

What steps can I take to avoid this scam? What if someone I know is already a victim? There are many steps you can take, some of which are proactive and some reactive, to help those loved ones in your life from being scammed. Here are some of them: (1) start a discussion about this scam by asking the senior what they would do if someone contacted them about winning a lottery. And be sure to warn them about this fraud. Let them know that international lotteries are illegal in the U.S.; (2) explain that you are concerned about their well-being. With their permission, monitor their financial accounts for unusual activity, review their phone logs for any unusual international calls, and look for any unusual incoming mail solicitations; (3) be aware of what's happening in their lives and any indicators of undue stress; (4) if they become a victim, then be supportive. Tell them, "It can happen to anyone;" and (5) finally, collect all documentation, make a copy, and report it to the authorities immediately.

In conclusion, it is certain that scammers will continue to use any and all means to tug at the heart strings and the purse strings of the elderly. By following the steps that I've just outlined, however, we can all make international lottery fraud less prevalent.

CHAPTER 4
Giving With Your Heart and Head

How do I know if a charity is legitimate? How do I know if a charity is worthy of my money? There are many virtues, including faith, hope, and wisdom. But the greatest virtue may be charity because it combines the love of self with the love of your neighbor and the love of Truth. The United States is the most charitable nation in the world. In 2015, Americans gave over $373 billion to charity, according to *CNN Money*. We give to charities that we are passionate about and that touch us, from those that fund cancer research to veteran support groups. Some charities are readily familiar – like the American Red Cross or the Salvation Army. Others are not. Whatever charity we give to, whether global or local, big or small, we should treat our donation like we would an investment, which means conducting research on the charity before we fork over our money. By all means give to charity, let your heart be your guide, and your head your guard. Let me demonstrate what I mean by telling you about a charity that contacted me in 2013.

In mid-July 2013 I received a call from the Association for Firefighters, Policemen, & Emergency Responders (AFPER)* (*I've changed their name). They wanted me to donate to them. According to *CNN*, a little less than two weeks earlier nineteen elite firefighters, members of the Prescott Fire Department's Granite Mountain Hotshots, were killed fighting a wildfire in Arizona. With that event still on my mind, how could I say "No"? I felt like I would be saying "No" to those fallen heroes. So I told the AFPER I would contribute to their cause. But I like to check out charities before giving to them. Besides, I don't give any personal information, including credit card or bank account numbers, over the phone when someone I don't know is calling me, so I told them that I'd like to send a check. That was acceptable, so I committed to giving $100. A few days later I received mail from the AFPER. They sent me a sponsor pledge form, a return envelope, and a sticker, which I haven't used yet.

Before writing the check, however, I got to work checking out this charity. First, I went to their website. According to that site, they help burn victims, provide funding to burn centers, and educate the public about burn and injury prevention. Elsewhere on the website it states: "Contributions made directly to AFPER are deposited in a special fund, in which 100% of the net revenue received is expended solely on program services." That sounded good to me. "But what does 'net revenue' mean?" I asked myself. In order to look into this further, I decided to access their Form 990 ("Return of Organization Exempt From Income Tax"), a form that all charities are required to file annually with the Internal Revenue Service. Basically, the 990 will show you how much money the charity has raised from the public, how they use that money, and any other expenses they have in operating the charity. In order to access their Form 990, I used a free online search tool provided by the New York State Attorney General's Office. I accessed the tool at https://www.charitiesnys.com. I had AFPER's Employer Identification Number ("EIN"), which was on their website, which made it easy for me to do the search. I could have also searched using their name. The latest Form 990 that was available was for calendar year 2011. (At that time, the 2012 form, which should have been filed by May 15th, assuming no extension, wasn't available yet.) The first page of AFPER's Form 990 told me all I needed to know.

Their "total revenue," mostly from contributions, was about $1.3 million. On the other hand, their grants (what they spend on program services, their mission, the reason they exist) was only $18,750. So, where did the rest of the money go? Let me examine that with you. Their salaries were nearly $71,000, almost four times the amount they spent on their mission. Most of the money, 90% of it, went to professional fundraisers. So now I know what "net revenue" means. It's the money they spend on grants after they pay the professional fundraiser, their salaries, and all other expenses. The bottom line is that if I honored my pledge of $100, $1.45 would have gone to a charitable cause. Actually, it is less than that, because some of their grants are provided to other charitable organizations that have expenses of their own, or are just as inefficient. Let me sum this up. This charity has been legally operating since 2002. Over the course of those years, very little has gone to fulfilling the charity's mission. Subsequent Form 990's relate a similar story. As of this writing, this charity's registration has been cancelled in New York State "because it failed to file its required annual financial reports with the Attorney General's Charities Bureau. As a result, this organization is prohibited from soliciting charitable contributions and grants in New York or engaging in any other charitable fundraising activities in New York," according to the information on this site: https://www.charitiesnys.com.

In 2003, the Supreme Court wrote in one of their unanimous decisions (*Illinois ex rel. Madigan v. Telemarketing Associates, Inc., Et. Al., 538 U.S. 600*) that the expenses of a charity, no matter how high, when properly disclosed, do not establish fraud. So it's left to us to determine the charities that are worthy of our hard-earned money and those that are not.

How can I be sure I'm making the most of my charitable contributions? There are simple steps you can take to better inform your charitable giving: (1) never give to a charity you don't know about on impulse, particularly after a recent tragedy, and especially if you are giving a large amount; (2) never give your credit card number, or other personal financial information, to a charity that you don't know to be legitimate; (2) don't be hesitant to ask the charity questions or for more information (such as their Form 990) before you give. Assess their level of cooperation. The best charities are transparent and accountable to the public; and (4) finally, conduct due diligence on the charity by reviewing the Form 990 or utilizing an online charity assessment tool, such as Charity Navigator (https://www.charitynavigator.org), which rates and provides summary information on over 5,000 charities, or, alternatively, GuideStar (https://www.guidestar.org). Both of these sites are free of charge and don't require you to register. These sites also offer resources to help you choose the right charity. Some charities have sent out solicitations where they prominently display the Charity Navigator rating, but it's wrong – they say it's four stars when it's actually three, so always go directly to Charity Navigator to see the most recent rating.

As of the time of this writing, the AFPER has a "Rating" of 0 stars on Charity Navigator. That means it's "Exceptionally Poor" and "Performs far below industry standards and below nearly all charities in its "Cause" category. Its Overall Score is 25.53 out of 100. Charity Navigator also includes comments about the charity from users. There were eleven comments, all negative, concerning the AFPER, including this comment from Ann Smith* (*I've changed her name) regarding the calls she had received from the charity's solicitors: "100% BS." I don't think she meant Boy Scouts. GuideStar didn't have any information on the AFPER.

While charities can be economically inefficient, they can also be outright frauds. Consider the case of Nouel Alba, who posed as the aunt of Noah Pozner, the youngest victim of the Sandy Hook Elementary School massacre. She pleaded guilty in June 2013 and was sentenced to eight months in prison and two years probation, according to *NBC Connecticut*. More recently, on

March 4, 2017, a man and woman were arrested for conning people in a charity scam. Part of the scam included using a photo of an ailing 5-year old from a legitimate GoFundMe page, according to *CBS New York*. Sometimes there's no limit to a fraudster's depravity.

In conclusion, according to https://www.foundationcenter.org, there are over one million charities in the United States. Many of these are worthy of our hard-earned money, others are not. Outright scams are certainly not. By following the four steps discussed above a decision on what charity to give to can be made easier. Don't rely just on faith or hope when giving. Use your wisdom. Give with your heart and head.

CHAPTER 5
Don't Take The Bait!

It was February 2011 and I had received an email from a current Facebook friend and former high school classmate – Kevin. The email was entitled "Sad News." My heart skipped a beat as I read on. According to the email, Kevin was in London for a short vacation with his family when he was mugged at gun point. They took his money, credit cards, and cell phone. He wrote that he was in tears. Kevin and his family were leaving London in three hours. He asked that I wire him $2,337.11 through Western Union and then email him back the money transfer control number, which he needed to pick up the money. He needed the money so he could pay his hotel bill before he left.

Then, I thought, some of this doesn't make sense. First, I hadn't seen Kevin in over 25 years and, while we were connected on Facebook, we hadn't communicated with each other much. Why would he come to me? Didn't he have closer family or friends? Second, I knew that he was a New York City Police Officer from his Facebook posts, and I just couldn't imagine one of New York's finest being in tears after being mugged. I could imagine him being angry about being mugged, perhaps, but not crying about it. Finally, his return email address was kevweiser1, but Weiser wasn't his last name. Why would he have such an unusual email address?

It turns out that the email didn't come from Kevin. It came from some unknown person from some unknown country who only wanted me to believe he was Kevin. This is known as email spoofing and it works hand in hand with phishing (pronounced like "fishing").

Phishing is a common internet-age scheme whereby a hacker attempts to acquire your personal information, such as username, password, and credit card data (and sometimes money) by masquerading as a trustworthy entity or, as in this case, a friend, in an electronic communication, be it email or an instant message. It typically works like this: (1) first, the hacker, by using malicious software ("malware"), obtains the email addresses of his targets. In my example, Kevin's Facebook account was compromised, probably because he clicked on an email link or attachment that he shouldn't have, causing the email addresses of all his friends to be stolen; (2) the hacker then sends out an email to each of the email addresses that he has stolen. The email appears to be from a legitimate company (like Facebook) or a legitimate friend (like Kevin), but it is not. The email requests that you to do something (e.g., typically, it's clicking on a link); (3) clicking on the link brings you to a fake webpage (e.g., "Faceboourk"), that looks very similar to the real one. You enter your personal information onto the fake page; and (4) finally, the hacker, who controls the fake webpage, will now take this personal information and use it himself or sell it to another crooked person.

According to https://www.emc.com, in 2012 there were over 400,000 phishing attacks worldwide, causing losses of about $1.5 billion. This effected over 37 million people, according to the *The Telegraph*. Anyone with a desktop computer, laptop, smartphone, or tablet is vulnerable to these types of attacks. Follow these steps to protect yourself: (1) never click on an embedded link or open an attachment from an unsolicited or unexpected email. If you can't verify the identity of the sender, then delete it without opening it. Independently go directly to the website you know by entering the address in the web browser and enter your login and password on a secure page. The internet address will start with "https" and an icon will be located to the right resembling a closed lock. Standard or nonsecure sites start with http. This stands for hypertext transfer (or transport) protocol and is the way the internet transfers data. The "s" in https means secure; (2) download any software or mobile device applications (or "apps") from reputable sources; (3) keep any of your application software up-to-date or remove it from your device. Third-party products such as Secunia or eEye Digital Security can quickly survey installed software and determine those needing patches or updates; (4) use a complex password on your devices and service accounts. Consider using a passphrase. Weak passwords, such as "123456" or "password," or default passwords, will make your systems vulnerable. Also, use a different password for each of the services you use on the Web. And change your passwords periodically; (5) make sure your device is installed with a comprehensive security suite with anti-virus, anti-phishing, and firewall capabilities. Keep these up-to-date; (6) when working in a wireless hotspot offered by coffee shops, hotels, or airports, then limit your activity to web browsing only. Avoid using banking websites or going to service accounts requiring a password; (7) avoid setting "out-of-office" messages on personal email accounts, as this can confirm to spammers that your email address is legitimate and can provide information to unknown parties about your activities; and (8) finally, avoid sending personal information through email or instant messaging.

In conclusion, there are many ways hackers try to get your personal information and/or money. Communications claiming to be from popular social websites, utility companies, or banks, among others are commonly used to lure the unsuspecting public. Follow the tips I mentioned to keep yourself protected. Hackers and other internet scammers will continue to attempt to phish for your information and money. Don't take the bait!

CHAPTER 6
Like Kin, But Less Than Kind

Looking around, we see that each of us, in some way or another, is connected to a group. For example, when I sit on the Long Island Rail Road taking the train from my town to New York City I'm part of the other commuters that do the same thing. I share a bond with these other commuters. It can be a bond that is forged by a shared frustration when the train is late, or not operating at all. Similarly, our interests, backgrounds, and other factors lead us to organizations that serve our needs. Those organizations can be a book or knitting club; a sports fantasy football league or golf tournament; a church or synagogue; or any ethnic congregation, such as a Chinese or Greek cultural center or community. When we share a common bond with others, we come to believe that each member of the group is similar to us in other aspects. For instance, we may view ourselves as decent and honest, so we assume that everyone else in the group is decent and honest. We base decisions on likeability and trust, rather than independent research and verification. Such careless decision-making may lead one to financial ruin.

There are many examples of those who have essentially said, "You can trust me because I'm like you. We share the same background and interests. And I can help you make money." Weizhen Tang, who was known as the "Chinese Warren Buffet" targeted the Chinese community in a $24 million dollar fraud. He billed himself as "the King of the 1% Weekly Returns." Jim and Tammy Faye Bakker targeted the religious community in a $190 million fraud. For $1,000, they sold "lifetime memberships" in a luxury resort that was never built. And Gary Davenport and three other accomplices targeted the elderly in a $2.5 million fraud. Davenport and his cohorts offered investors "guaranteed" promissory notes. Each of these fraudsters went beyond the common bond that they had with an ethnic, religious, or age-based group by developing such a close rapport and strong relationship with the group that the group trusted them like family. These con men then took advantage of this trust by stealing, through deception, the community's hard earned money. They were like kin, but less than kind. They each pulled off an affinity fraud.

An affinity fraud, a term that was created in the late 1980s by journalists and regulators, according to *Fraud*, is an investment scam that is pulled off against members of a particular group, such as a religious, ethnic, professional, or age-based group. Each of these groups is united by common traits that create inherent trust. The three most common affinity groups targeted by investment scammers are the elderly or retired, religious groups, and ethnic groups, respectively.

There are many steps you can take to avoid becoming a victim of affinity fraud. Here are some of them: (1) don't rush into investment decisions. You've spent a lifetime earning your savings, so spend some time to understand the investment; (2) get as much information as possible in writing. Ask for a prospectus or offering document. Independently determine if the investment has been registered with federal or state regulators. For the Securities and Exchange Commission, which is the federal regulator, check out https://www.edgar.gov, and for a state regulator call its investor protection bureau. (For example, for New York, it's the Investor Protection Bureau of the Office of the New York State Attorney General, which can be reached at 212-416-8222.); (3) stay away if the investment is described as "risk free," "guaranteed," or "a sure thing;" (4) ask what firm will hold your investment and money. Insist on a separate account in your name at a qualified and reputable third-party custodian. It should be with a recognizable and established institution, which independently provides you with independent account statements; (5) check out the individual making the investment pitch and his company. Individual investment advisors or brokers, and their firms, are required to be registered. You can check them out using FINRA BrokerCheck, an online tool at https://brokercheck.finra.org, or with the state's investor protection bureau; and (6) don't put all your eggs in one basket. Diversify your investments.

Affinity frauds are rampant. As recently as March 30, 2017, the SEC brought fraud charges, in the form of a complaint, against Larry Holley, a Michigan-based pastor who exploited church members, including retirees. Holley, claiming he was more trustworthy than a banker, "cloaked his solicitations in faith-based rhetoric," according to the SEC. Through his company – Treasure Enterprise LLC – and with a business associate, Holley raised about $6.7 million from more than 80 investors who were guaranteed high returns and told they were investing in a profitable real estate company with hundreds of residential and commercial properties, according to the complaint. Holley's business, which wasn't registered to sell investments, struggled and was unable to pay investors, according to the SEC. "As alleged in our complaint, Holley and [his associate] targeted the retirement savings of churchgoers, building a bond of trust purportedly based on faith but actually based on false promises," said David Glockner, Director of the SEC's Chicago Regional Office.

In conclusion, beware of the wolf in sheep's clothing. They are like kin, but less than kind. They ingratiate themselves with the group in order to carry out an investment scam. The decision to make an investment should never be based solely on trust. To protect yourself from these investment scams, understand and research not only the investment, but those who recommend the investment.

CHAPTER 7
RoboCop For Robocallers?

The incessant and annoying calls asking, "Can you hear me now?" can be frustrating. How do we stop them? Do we need a RoboCop for robocallers? If your phone rings and the caller ID shows a number you don't know, don't answer it. Many are "spoofed robocalls," i.e., robocalls where the caller ID is faked, hiding the caller's true identity. According to the Federal Trade Commission, a federal consumer protection agency, these pre-recorded calls are illegal. They are also the biggest source of complaints at the FTC, increasing considerably since 2009, according to *The Columbus Dispatch*. One of the reasons for the growth is that making these calls has become cheaper and easier, because of the improved technology, according to the *Dispatch*. Not to be outdone by its sister agency, the Federal Communication Commission says that robocalls and telemarketing calls are consistently the top source of consumer complaints that it receives. The FCC is a federal agency that regulates phone communications, among other things. It is estimated that U.S. consumers received approximately 2.4 billion robocalls per month in 2016.

A few years ago, ceaseless calls were being made by telemarketers about a worthless car warranty. They went something like this: "This is the final notice that the factory warranty on your vehicle may have expired, and should be reactivated to protect you against the cost of repairs. If you have not responded to this notification, it's not too late. Please don't make the mistake of driving without a warranty. You are still eligible to reactivate warranty coverage. This is the final call before we close the file. Press one to speak with a representative now about your vehicle."

At the time the Better Business Bureau (BBB), which has

been working since 1912 to uphold a "marketplace where buyers and sellers can trust each other," reported that it handled almost 5,000 complaints against companies attempting to sell auto warranties in the manner described above. The BBB concluded that even if consumers decide to get the warranty, they include so many restrictive terms that the warranty may prove to be worthless. It seems that no one is spared the calls. Alison Southwick, a BBB spokeswoman, told *Fox News*, "Personally, I receive these calls all the time, and I don't even own a car." Telemarketing companies targeted or banned in one state can simply move to another state. Having the FTC tackle the issue would prevent this "state hopping" practice. Unfortunately, the telemarketers making these calls are difficult, if not impossible, to identify.

So what can consumers do? The best thing to do is not answer the call. If you don't recognize the number, it's probably illegitimate. If not, then any legitimate caller will leave a message. If you do answer such a call then take these steps: (1) don't respond or press any numbers, which will certainly lead to more calls from the same, and other, scammers; (2) hang up; (3) contact your telephone provider to see what they can offer to block these unwanted calls. The FCC has encouraged the major telecommunications carriers to offer cost-free call-blocking services to customers; (4) put your phone number on the "Do Not Call" registry. Access the registry here: https://www.donotcall.gov/ or by calling 1-888-382-1222. Callers who don't respect the "Do Not Call" rules are more likely to be crooks; and (5) file a complaint with the FTC here: https://www.ftccomplaintassistant.gov/Details#crnt or call 1-877-382-4357.

In March 2017 the FCC issued a proposal that is designed to weaken the ability of scammers to utilize spoofed robocalls. Consumer groups, the telecommunications industry, and the federal government are determined to stop these calls. In order to do that, they are proposing making it permissible for telephone service providers to block spoofed robocalls. Specifically, the proposal would allow providers to block such calls when the subscriber to a particular telephone number requests that calls originating from that number be blocked (sometimes called "Do-Not-Originate") and when the spoofed Caller ID can't possibly be valid, including numbers that haven't been assigned to anyone yet, according to the FCC. In addition, the FCC is seeking comment on (1) how to address spoofing from internationally-originated numbers, where scammers often hide to avoid U.S. legal processes; (2) how to create a "safe harbor" for providers from their FCC-imposed call completion obligations when they rely on objective criteria to prevent fraudulent, illegal, or spoofed robocalls from reaching consumers; and (3) safeguards the FCC should put in place to minimize blocking of lawful calls. The proposal was derived from the work of a Robocall Strike Force set-up by the FCC, and consisting of telecommunications industry companies, including AT&T, Google, Microsoft, and, Verizon. Also, in March 2017, T-Mobile – a Robocall Strike Force participant – announced that it would warn recipients of potential scam calls by showing the caller ID as "scam likely." T-Mobile said that its service works by comparing phone numbers to its list of known scammers. Their database is constantly updated by analyzing call patterns.

Evolution of the Do-Not Call Registry

Telephone Consumer Protection Act (TCPA) of 1991 and its accompanying FCC regulations. Restricts the use of automated telephone dialing systems; prevents telemarketers from calling you before 8 a.m. or after 9 p.m. your local time; and requires telemarketers to maintain a "Do Not Call" list.

Do-Not-Call Implementation Act of 2003. Created the National "Do Not Call" registry. Phone numbers were required to remain on the list for five years. The "Do Not Call" registry does not limit calls by political organizations, charities, or telephone surveyors. Note that scammers first pose as surveyors to get personal information from you, for purposes of setting up future calls.

Controlling the Assault of Non-Solicited Pornography and Marketing (CAN-SPAM) Act of 2003. Prohibits telemarketers from sending junk-mail, i.e., spam, to wireless devices, such as your mobile phone, without prior permission.

Do-Not-Call Improvement Act of 2007. Required that phone numbers permanently remain on the national "Do Not Call" registry.

CHAPTER 8
Investigate Before You Invest

I just want to say one word to you. Just one word. Are you listening? *"Lithium."* Lithium, from the Greek word *lithos* meaning stone, is a soft, silver-white metal. Its Periodic Table of the Elements symbol is Li. It is used to make many things, including car and smartphone batteries, medicines, and telescope lenses. In fiction, it powered Star Trek's USS Enterprise. Lithium is the fuel of the future. So, you can only imagine my excitement when in May 2011 the "StockMarketAuthority" sent me a glossy brochure telling me I could turn $10,000 into $100,000 by investing in a company called Lithium Exploration Group (LEXG). Now, let's see how well this $10,000 investment has done. A $10,000 investment in LEXG in May 2011, when I received this brochure, would have been worth $385 in late July 2013. At the time of this writing it is worth $5.88. I would have lost nearly all my investment. That's, of course, before factoring in the fees and other transactions costs I would have had to pay my broker.

The good news is that I didn't let my excitement get in the way of being patient and doing research on this company. It took a lot of hard work for me to earn $10,000, so it made sense for me to spend some time to do some investigating before I invested.

I took three steps in researching this investment. The first thing I did was go back to the brochure. Remember, the brochure came from the StockMarketAuthority. Recall that one of the methods criminals use is to make it seem that they are in a position of authority, so that they can get you to listen to them with rapt attention, putting yourself in an inferior, subservient position. One page in the brochure stated, "Time is of the essence." Any investment pitch that stresses urgency is a red flag that may indicate a scam. Then I went to the fine print in the brochure. I could barely see it, but the words you can barely see, are the words you want to read, that you need to read. This fine print disclosure states that the StockMarketAuthority has neither conducted research on LEXG nor are they recommending you buy this stock. They could have fooled me! In addition, Gekko Industries, an offshore company that owns stock in Lithium Exploration Group, paid for this advertising. That was a clear conflict of interest. Moreover, sometimes criminals like to get cute. Those behind the StockMarketAuthority were no exception. Gordon *Gekko* was a fictional character in Oliver Stone's *Wall Street*. Gekko was a corporate takeover artist with questionable ethics who was eventually convicted of insider trading.

I didn't need further information to conclude that this was a likely "pump and dump" scheme. Gekko, or the people behind it, paid for the ad in order to attract buyers who would boost, or "pump" up, the price of the stock. Gekko, or other individuals or entities colluding with Gekko, would then eventually sell, or dump, its stock at inflated prices. Once promoters like Gekko "dump" their stock, prices eventually fall and investors lose their money

There was no way I was going to invest in this company. Although I was sure of my conclusion, I continued my analysis. I went to Yahoo Finance to get a price quote and see where this stock trades. Based on the price and the trading venue, it was clear that this company was a penny stock. A penny stock is the stock of a very small, highly speculative company that trades for less than $5 per share. Penny stocks don't trade on a national stock exchange, like the New York Stock Exchange or Nasdaq. They can't because they don't meet the exchanges' listing standards. They don't even come close. Rather, they trade on

what is known as the OTCMarkets
(https://www.otcmarkets.com), which has different
marketplaces with different standards. While not all companies
on the OTC Markets are obscure, financially-struggling
companies (in fact, some are well-known, legitimate companies),
the solicitations that investors tend to receive in the mail, or in
their email, are of companies that tend to be categorized in the
more troubling areas of this marketplace. For example,
companies with a *YIELD* sign, meaning "Pink Sheet –Limited
Information," have financial reporting problems, are in
economic distress, or even worse – bankruptcy. They make
limited information publicly available. This also includes
companies that while not necessarily troubled, are unwilling to
provide disclosure, which should be troubling to any investor.
Further, there are companies with a *STOP* sign, meaning "Pink
Sheet – No Information," which means companies that do not
provide disclosures, financial or otherwise, to their investors.
OTCMarkets warns, "Publicly traded companies that do not
provide information to investors should be carefully researched
before making any investment decision." Believe it or not, it gets
worse. Some securities are designated with a *skull and crossbones*,
as are bottles of poison. OTCMarkets warns investors that
"there may be reason to exercise additional care and perform
thorough due diligence before making an investment decision"
in these "Caveat Emptor" ("Buyer Beware" in Latin) securities.
Great advice. If you want to commit financial hara-kiri, by all
means indulge. Your best bet may be to stay away.

Finally, I reviewed LEXG's most recent Form 10-K, which
was dated June 30, 2010. A Form 10-K is a comprehensive
report that includes a public company's business description and
financial performance that must be submitted annually to the
Securities and Exchange Commission, which is a U.S.
government stock market and public company regulator. I

obtained the Form 10-K from the SEC's website – http://www.sec.gov. The Form 10-K indicated that LEXG has no revenue, no profits, and negative stockholders' equity, which means its liabilities, what it owes, exceed its assets, what it owns. The independent auditor report, which is part of the Form 10-K, indicated that the company has lost money year after year and questioned its ability to continue operating.

Just in case you think this was an unusual incident, consider that I received several other pieces of literature from these penny stock companies through the U.S. Postal Service. Between mid-2011 and mid-2015, I received fifteen pieces of sales literature beyond the one for LEXG. Of these, all would have lost me money as of the time of this writing, had I invested in them. Most of them lost all their value. A hypothetical investment of $10,000 in each security for which I received a solicitation, for a total outlay of $160,000, would have fallen to $11,507.

Not only do I receive these solicitations through "snail" mail, but email, as well. From late 2013 through late 2016 I had received 13 distinct solicitations. Most were of stock trading on the OTCMarkets. A few have lost all of their value, some 80% or more, and one gained about 11%, although it's extremely volatile. These figures are before transaction costs and assume that the security would have been purchased at a favorable price after receipt of the solicitation. Another security that I received a solicitation on, inexplicably, was the well-known, and well-regarded, Apple Inc. (AAPL), which is listed on the Nasdaq Stock Market. It rose 103%, as of the time of this writing. A hypothetical investment of $10,000 in each security for which I received a solicitation, for a total outlay of $130,000, would have fallen to $39,805 (even with Apple Inc. in the portfolio). One of the solicitations in email came from "Jimmy The Chop." I don't know about you, but generally I don't like to do business with people whose middle name is "The."

Not only can solicitations come through mail and email, but from "inadvertent" telephone messages left on your voicemail. In 2006 the U.S. attorney for the District of Columbia criminally charged a trio who were involved in this "wrong number" scheme in which a caller identifying herself as "Debbie" wanted to pass along to a girlfriend a "hot" stock tip from a "hot stock exchange guy" she was dating. The trio expected innocent recipients to buy the securities, and they did. As reported by *Fox News*, it drove up the combined market value of six small-company stocks by about $179 million in just 26 days, according to government officials.

Oil and gas, or mineral, exploration are areas wherein scams are likely to occur in regard to "penny stocks" or "microcap securities" because it's hard to verify the existence of the underlying assets the company purports to possess. Certainly, a typical investor who doesn't have training in geology, would be hard pressed to find out. Microcap securities are those smaller companies with a market capitalization of less than $250 or $300 million, according to the SEC. Those companies, with market capitalizations of less than $50 million, are sometimes referred to as "nanocap securities." A company's market capitalization is the number of common shares it has outstanding multiplied by its market price. Sometimes the *market capitalization* of a company becomes very far removed from its *balance sheet capitalization*. Capitalization, which is obtained from a company's Balance Sheet, is: *"Common Stock" (par value)* + *"Long-Term Debt"* + *"Retained Earnings" or - "Accumulated Deficit."*

While a company's *market capitalization* can never go below 0, *balance sheet capitalization* can, especially if the company has built up an "Accumulated Deficit," which would come from losing money year after year.

Fraudsters are now getting stocks to more than $5, either through manipulative means or by conducting reverse stock splits, so that the stock doesn't have the taint of being categorized as a "penny stock." A reverse stock split occurs when a public company reduces the total number of its outstanding shares. An example is as follows: if a company has 200 million shares outstanding and the shares are trading at $2 each, a 1-for-10 reverse split would reduce the number of shares to 20 million, while the shares should trade at about $20. The company's market capitalization should, at least theoretically, remain unchanged at $400 million at the time of the split. Of course, the market capitalization will deviate with the share price's volatility afterward. In other words, stock prices move.

There are steps you can take to protect yourself from these "pump and dump" schemes: (1) be wary of unsolicited stock offers no matter how they get to you, whether through email or mail, telephone, or social media, such as Facebook or Twitter; (2) don't rush into a stock investment or any other investment. Take the time to carefully and thoroughly research the investment, particularly the risks of the investment, before investing. Don't forget to read the fine print; and (3) if you don't have the time to research investments yourself, then consult with an independent and trusted financial advisor or broker.

In conclusion, investments are capitalism's fuel. And capitalism is one of the things that make America great. Our personal wealth, however, is too precious to leave to the whims of our excitement and impatience. And our wealth should not be wasted on these "pump and dump" schemes. Investigate before you invest.

CHAPTER 9
Robbing Peter to Pay Paul

In 1919 the 37-year old Charles Ponzi, a confident, dapper, and jaunty Italian immigrant, hit upon an idea concerning international reply coupons (IRCs), which were introduced in 1906 (well before air mail) and allowed holders to exchange them for one or more postage stamps that could be used to send a priority letter up to a certain weight overseas. So, if a brother in the U.S. wrote to his sister in France, let's say, and wanted her to reply, then he would purchase an IRC and enclose it in the envelope with his letter. She, in turn, would go to her local post office and exchange the IRC for stamps. The process worked in reverse as well, so the sister could purchase an IRC in France and mail it to her brother in the U.S.

Because the U.S. dollar strengthened against European currencies, including the French franc and Italian lira, after World War I, while IRCs still bought the same amount of stamps, Ponzi figured he could, for example, send dollars to Italy, have his contacts in Italy exchange the dollars for lira, then purchase IRCs with the lira that would be mailed to the US. The IRC, once in the US, would be used to purchase stamps that would then be sold at a discount. Because of the change in exchange rates pre to post-WWI, the $1 went from buying 5 lira to 20 lira, so you could buy more IRCs with lira then with dollars. Again, however, the IRCs still bought the same amount of stamps.

Ponzi's International Reply Coupon Scheme

Step 1: Send $1 to Italy

Step 2: Exchange $1 for £20

Step 3: £20 would purchase about 66 IRCs

Step 4: Send the 66 IRCs to the U.S.

Step 5: Exchange the IRCs for stamps worth about $3.30

Step 6: Sell the stamps for a 10% discount or $3, netting $2

Theoretically, on this transaction, Ponzi would make $2 or a 200% profit margin.

Ponzi told a *Boston Post* reporter, "I investigated the rate of exchange in many of the other foreign countries. My original theory, 'Why can't I make money this way?' grew more real. Then it became a fact." It sounded good, so he figured he could take investor money and increase the scale of the operation. Of course he'd have to pay a return to those investors, and commissions to the salespeople he planned to hire. So, in January 1920 he started the Security and Exchange Company (not to be confused with today's Securities and Exchange Commission, which was created in 1934 to protect investors) at 27 School Street in Boston's North End. He oozed success, even keeping a certified check for $1 million in his jacket pocket, visible for all to see. He also surrounded himself with successful people – a distinguished lawyer and public relations man, who only gave him more credibility. These patinas of a prosperous company, as well as the success that the early investors would have, attracted all classes of Bostonians to his venture, like bees to honey.

While the arbitrage opportunity Ponzi cooked up might have worked on a small scale, there was no way, logistically, it was going to work on a large one. He promised investors, through his prospectus, returns of 50% over 45 days, and 100% over 90 days. Any money that investors paid-in to this scheme was held by Ponzi, who lived a lavish lifestyle. Those investors that got out early did see returns and, because they did, validated Ponzi's operation, while those that waited lost their money. Essentially, the money that investors put in later was used to pay returns to the earlier investors. In the end, this scheme cost thousands of investors $20 million (about

$243 million today). Six banks failed because of his chicanery. In retrospect, there were many red flags that could have alerted investors to Ponzi's scheme: (1) his in-laws wouldn't lend him money for a business venture; (2) he put his own money in the bank where it earned about 1/10th of what he was offering his investors; and (3) most importantly, he had been previously arrested and jailed for three years for forgery. This "Robbing Peter to Pay Paul" tactic, around since as early as the 16th century, would henceforth be known as the "Ponzi scheme."

The Ponzi scheme is still alive and well, and prospering, long after its namesake's prison term, and death in 1949. And the Ponzi schemer can be young or old, male or female, black or white, college-educated or not. They are of all stripes, but have in common a mischievous tongue, cunning manner, and devious purpose. Just in February 2017, a New York attorney brought a suit against someone he met in court who was seeking legal advice, only to take him for $30,000 in an investment opportunity; a 70-year old Michigan woman was sentenced to seventy months in prison for bilking investors, some of whom put in their entire retirement savings, out of $7.5 million; and a former president of Sleepy's, the U.S. mattress chain, said he and several trusts lost $1.5 million in a "can't lose" investment scheme. There are many other recent Ponzi schemes, some of which are still going on, but haven't been reported yet. As of March 2017, the global financial markets are doing relatively well. As such, Ponzi schemes tend to be hidden for longer. They tend to be uncovered when the financial markets and the economy unravel. That was the case with the most well-known one – Bernie Madoff's $50 billion investment scheme. Madoff's fraud, as well as several others, were uncovered in the midst of the 2007-2009 Global Financial Crisis. Including Madoff, who confessed, Nicholas Cosmo (founder of Agape World) was caught in a $380 million investment fraud and Tom Petters in a

$3.65 billion Ponzi scheme that bilked investors over a thirteen-year period. Are you sitting on an investment that will be exposed during the next crisis? Don't wait to find out. Start asking questions, reading the documentation, if there is any, and ascertaining where the money you forked over is and who controls it. Even if you're being paid periodically, you need to ask questions. For example: "Is the money I'm being paid monthly coming from the principal I paid in?"

Many Ponzi schemes may start off with good intentions, but you know about the road to hell. On April 20, 2017 *North Shore News*, which covers news from Vancouver, British Columbia, reported that Virginia Tan admitted to fraudulently raising at least $30 million between 2011 and 2015 in a Ponzi scheme. It appears that Tan started off with a legitimate operation. She ran a business that involved making short-term, high interest loans to individuals and small businesses that were unable to obtain traditional financing from financial institutions." At some point, though, she discontinued the business, but continued raising funds from investors. Doug Muir, director of enforcement for the B.C. Securities Commission, without specifically referring to the facts and circumstances of this case states that sometimes Ponzi schemes start with a legitimate business, but then the operation runs amok, operators get in over their heads, and "it morphs into a fraudulent scheme," he said.

According to North American Securities Administrators Association (NASAA), which is the oldest international organization devoted to investor protection, Ponzi schemes have been perpetrated by the following: a 23-year-old Ohio busboy. He raised $7.3 million from 2,800 investors by promising to double their money in two or three months. The funds were supposed to be used to buy rock concert tickets in bulk and resell them at high prices; an Alabama man who fleeced investors of $3.5 million in a blue jeans resale scheme; a Texas woman who took in $17 million to finance a chain of phony silver recycling plants; and a Utah funeral home organist who bilked widows of $16.5 million by promising to invest their money in high-interest paying bonds of a nonexistent finance company. Others Ponzi schemers have included: Sarah Howe, who created a Ladies' Deposit Fund in the later 19th century promising 8% interest and Clelia Flores, who operated a fraudulent investment scheme, promising returns of up to 25% within 30 to 45 days. This fraudulent strategy attracted more than 150 investors in seven states between late 2006 and early 2008. Investors purportedly put their money in risk-free, high-yield investment programs in real estate, commodities, and bank instrument trading. Flores, however, used new investor money to pay earlier investors, and misappropriated other investor money to pay for her personal expenses. If these people have such great ideas on how to make money, then why do they come to you, for your money, why don't they use their own?

Even if an investment is legitimate, brokers or advisors can fail to do their job. Advisors are required to keep your best interests in mind when investing on your behalf. Brokers, on the other hand, are required to make sure any investments they recommend to you are suitable, given your age, income, tolerance for risk, etc. Before selecting a broker or advisor, ask them lots of questions. The SEC provides a list here: https://www.sec.gov/reportspubs/investor-publications/investorpubsaskquestionshtm.html Once you select an advisor or broker, they should be asking you lots of questions and getting to know you and your financial situation thoroughly before investing your money or making recommendations. If they don't, then they're not doing their job. That's a red flag.

This is what the senior can do (before the scam): (1) don't

rush into investment decisions. You've spent a lifetime earning your savings, so spend some time understanding the investment; (2) don't use unsolicited emails, message board postings, company news releases, or personal investment tips (even from a family member or a trusted friend) as the sole basis for your investment decisions; (3) ask lots of questions and check out the answers; (4) get as much information as possible in writing. Ask for a prospectus or offering document. Ask for any promises in writing. Be wary of an investment opportunity that isn't in writing; (5) understand the risks of the investments you make. Higher returns come with higher risks. Are these risks being disclosed to you? Are you willing to bear them?; (6) review and complete any account opening documents carefully and completely. Read the documents before you sign. Keep copies for yourself; (7) be wary if you are told to keep the investment opportunity confidential; (8) be wary of foreign or offshore investments. It's more difficult to determine if these are legitimate; (9) stay away if the investment is described as "no risk," "risk free," "guaranteed," or "a sure thing"; (10) investigate the person introducing the investment opportunity and the investment opportunity itself. Verify information with independent sources. Are they licensed? Is the investment product registered? Investigate the broker or advisor, their firm, and the investment – all three – before you invest. Check out brokers or advisors and their firms here: https://brokercheck.finra.org. Check out public companies or registered investments (e.g., mutual funds or variable insurance products) here: http://www.sec.gov/edgar/searchedgar/webusers.htm. Check out investments with your state's investor protection bureau; (11) if a product is not registered with the Securities and Exchange Commission (SEC) – the federal securities regulator – or a state securities regulator or is not specifically, and legitimately, exempt from registration, then this may be a scam; (12) be wary of certain professional designations, such as "Senior Specialist" or

"Retirement Advisor." Some of these designations are relatively easy to obtain; (13) don't feel indebted to a broker or advisor. They work for you; (14) be wary of those who stress urgency, e.g., "You need to do this right now" or "This is a once in a lifetime offer and will be gone tomorrow"; (15) never give your broker full discretion. For example, there's no reason that your broker should have control of moving your cash out of your account; (16) don't be fooled by a professional looking website. Websites can be easy and fairly cheap to create; (17) ask what firm will hold your investment and money. Insist on a separate account in your name at a third-party custodian. It should be with a recognizable and established institution, one that independently provides you with account statements. Custodians only hold assets – cash or securities. They don't evaluate the quality or legitimacy of any investment; (18) monitor the activity in your account regularly. You should be receiving regular account statements (at least quarterly, if not monthly). You should also be able to review daily activity if you have online access; (19) don't invest in an opportunity you don't fully understand and know to be legitimate; (20) don't put all your eggs in one basket. Diversify your investments.

This is what the senior can do (after the scam): (1) file a complaint with the SEC here: http://www.sec.gov/complaint/select.shtml or with the Financial Industry Regulatory Authority (FINRA) – the self-regulatory organization for the securities industry – here: http://www.finra.org/Investors/ProtectYourself/p118628

FINRA also has a toll-free Helpline For Seniors that can be called to get assistance regarding issues with brokerage accounts and investments. You can call 1-844-574-3577, Monday to Friday, 9 a.m. to 5 p.m. Eastern Daylight Time.

CHAPTER 10
Wooed By A Website

An elderly acquaintance of mine – Lena Jarrow* (*I've changed her name) – was convinced by a scammer, after much beguiling, to put most of her life savings into an overseas venture. He guaranteed her that by signing a promissory note and forking over the money, she'd make a 10% return. The fraudster convinced her to invest after wining and dining her, and then showing her his company's favorable press coverage, as well as its impressive website. Lena felt regret within days of handing over the check. It was too late to stop payment on it. Although she never got her money back, she did report the fraud to the authorities. One of the most puzzling aspects of financial crimes, like the one Lena experienced, is that victims fail to report it. They may try to convince themselves that the fraud didn't take place. If they accept it took place, then they might have to accept that they're not capable of good judgment, which would damage their pride. Once you've realized you've been defrauded, you might be too embarrassed to admit it or you may not bother to report it to the proper authorities because you don't feel it will do any good. It takes courage to admit you were wrong, to come forward publicly, and to try to prevent others from being taken advantage of. Victims are not stupid, they are manipulated precisely because they are honest and decent, and only expected the same from their fellow citizens. Lena showed her honesty and decency, and courage. She has learned from her experience, and wants others to learn from it as well. In addition to reporting the fraud to the authorities, she even complained to the alleged fraudster's bank. By doing so she may have gotten his bank thinking about filing a Suspicious Activity Report (SAR) against him. A SAR is a document that financial institutions are required to file with the government when they suspect fraud has been committed by one of their customers. Signing your name on a piece of paper, as Lena did, is painless. She realizes now that she should have conducted due diligence on the company beforehand. If she did so, she would have quickly realized it was a fraud. Facts can be checked out. Promises, however, cannot. The North American Securities Administrators Association (NASAA), the international investor protection organization, lists "[u]nregistered products/unlicensed salesmen" first in its list of "Top Investor Threats," and promissory notes are second. Says NASAA, "Legitimate promissory notes are marketed almost exclusively to sophisticated or corporate investors with the resources…" needed to do the required due diligence. The alleged fraudster in Lena's case wasn't running a Ponzi scheme, like the infamous Madoff did, where money from new investors is paid to previous ones, with the intent to expand the number of investors who are impressed with the investment returns. He was a hit-and-run con artist who absconded with her money. The money went on a one-way trip whose destination was the bank account controlled by the fraudster to be spent on his lavish lifestyle. He doesn't impress with false investment returns, but rather with a sophisticated and professional demeanor, and fancy suits, watches, and cars to match. Also, like the Navy's "Sea Shadow" ship, this alleged fraudster is able to evade the prosecutor's radar, perhaps because he's not too greedy, raising only a relatively small amount of money, and he's operating within one state, yet not having a physical business presence in the state.

Lessons Learned

Be Skeptical When Being Promised "Guaranteed Income" or a "Guaranteed Return." "Con artists…try to bypass stringent state registration requirements to pitch unregistered investments with a promise of 'limited or no risk' and high returns," says NASAA. The Securities and Exchange Commission (SEC), a federal agency whose mission is to protect the investing public, in a podcast entitled "'Guaranteed' High Returns," stated, "… you know that crooks talk about 'guaranteed' high returns to try to sucker you into sending them your money. We've devoted whole podcasts to telling you to run, not walk from people who tell you a high return is 'can't miss' or 'guaranteed.'" Listen to the SEC's advice, and run as fast as you can, from these too good to be true financial traps. Remember, there are only two things that are guaranteed – death and taxes.

Higher Return Means Higher Risk. One of the basic tenets of investing is that higher returns come with higher risks. If someone is promising you a 10% return when the risk-free rate (that is, the interest rate on a 3-month U.S. Treasury bill) is less than 1%, then you can be sure that you're taking much greater risk. If you're being told there is no risk, then at best someone is misrepresenting the investment or at worst it's a scam.

Short-Term Doesn't Necessarily Mean Risk-Free. If you are investing in a short-term, i.e., 3-month, U.S. Treasury security, then that's considered risk-free. But, not all investments that are short-term are risk free. Someone may promise you a significant return over a short period of time. Remember Charles Ponzi's promise of a 50% return over 45 days. However, don't let the short-term nature of the investment period fool you.

Be Patient When Selecting an Investment, and Don't Feel Pressured to Invest Immediately. Invariably, investment scams lay the groundwork for getting investors to move quickly before they do any critical thinking. Take your time and ask the questions you need to. Be like Gary Cooper's Longfellow Deeds character in the Frank Capra-directed *Mr. Deeds Goes to Town.* Shortly after Mr. Deeds, a country bumpkin who enjoys playing the tuba so he can think, inherits $20 million from his uncle, he's pressured by his lawyers to sign a power of attorney that would allow them to manage the money without any further fees beyond what they've already charged for the legal work. Mr. Deeds responds, as follows: "It puzzles me why these people all would want to work for nothing. It isn't natural. So, I guess I better think about it some more." Mr. Deeds may be unsophisticated, but he's also patient, inquisitive, skeptical, and tough. About the inheritance, Mr. Deeds says, "I expect to do a lot of good with that money, and I can't afford to put it into anything I don't look into." You don't have to learn to play the tuba to help you think about an investment. Take a walk, do some knitting, tend to the garden. The point is to think and wait, and stand your ground. Any legitimate individual will give you the time you need to figure it out.

Be Aware That a Company Can Have a Fake Website. Today, there are a surfeit of tools to create an impressive and impactful website, one that may make the company seem bigger than it actually is, perhaps like a global behemoth. When you look at a website of a company you're contemplating investing in, do look at it like you can't see the forest for the trees. Look at the details in the website. If it's fraudulent, then you'll be able to break down the lies, one by one.

Be Aware That Companies Can Issue Fake Press Releases. It's relatively easy to set-up a company and issue a press release, and the press release can say whatever you want it to, even if it's not the truth. This typically happens with smaller companies, whether private or public, with either no audited financial information in the public domain or audited financials that show little or no revenue. The press release can make false claims about financials, including revenue or profits, a new product launch, a government patent or drug approval, or just about anything that's positive in order to move the security's price (if it's a publicly traded company) or to have an investor fork over his hard earned money (if it's a privately available investment opportunity).

Don't Take What Is Written At Face Value When It Doesn't Come From a Well-Known, Widely-Circulated

Publication. Back in 1987, Benjamin Mark Cole, a well-regarded reporter who wrote *The Pied Pipers of Wall Street : How Analysts Sell You Down the River*, worked for the *Los Angeles Business Journal.* In one of the many articles he wrote, there was one within which he tried to convey a lesson to business journalists. "Reporters and editors can be duped by a good relations blitz. And when journalists are hoodwinked, they help to promote, not expose, shabby operators," he wrote. Bre-X Minerals Ltd., which was a publicly-listed Canadian company that started business in 1989, reported having significant gold deposits, which caused its stock to rise. It was a fraud that collapsed in 1997. The gold holdings didn't exist. The Bre-X fraud was dependent on "journalists who took the bait" (in the form of false press releases) who "were generally inexperienced and hungry for a good story that could make their name" (in other words, genuine fake news), according to Tom Ajamie and Bruce Kelly who wrote *Financial Serial Killers.* One such reporter who fell for the Bre-X spiel "expressed regret for his role in promoting the scam, according to Ajamie and Kelly. James Gordon Bennett, the founder of the *New York Herald* once said, "…many a good story has been ruined by over- verification." You don't want a good story, you want the facts, so do as much verifying as you need to in order to come to a prudent and informed decision.

Make Important Decisions in Solitude, Not In the Tumult of the Moment. When making an investment decision, it important that you certainly seek the advice of those you trust, including close family and friends, but any final decision that concerns your money, should be made deliberately. Certainly don't make the decision during a dinner with someone you've known only for a short time, like my acquaintance Lena did.

CHAPTER 11
Fraud Is Infinite In Variety

Fraud goes back to the beginning of time. It goes as far back as the Garden of Eden, and Adam, Eve, and the Serpent. We've presented many common scams in the earlier chapters of this book. Lord Macnaghten, a famous jurist in 19th century England, said that "fraud is infinite in variety." There are many scams. Constantly, and importantly, existing ones are being refined and new ones created. Fraudsters are always revising and trying to perfect their schemes. Below is a non-exhaustive list.

Automated Teller Machine (ATM) Scam

The scammer may try to read your personal identification number (PIN) by "shoulder surfing" or using a hidden camera while capturing ("skimming") your card number by using a counterfeit reader placed over the ATM slot.

Here are some tips: (1) look around; beware of shoulder surfers; (2) use ATMs from established banks in well-trafficked areas; (3) block the keyboard when entering your personal identification number (PIN); (4) if you request a receipt, then take the receipt with you. If you're going to discard the receipt, then tear it up and discard it at home; (5) never write your PIN on your ATM card or on any piece of paper in your wallet; (6) don't use more obvious PIN numbers, such as your street address number, the first or last 4 digits of your social security number, or your birth date. Many people use these obvious numbers, which the criminal can easily deduce; and (7) review your bank statement for unusual activity; report any unusual activity to your bank immediately.

Bereavement Scam (a.k.a. Obituary Scam)

The scammer reads obituaries, whether in the newspaper or online, and then approaches the widow/widower and claims the deceased owed them money. Refer them to the executor or attorney handling the estate, who should verify the debt by going through the deceased's financial records.

Gas Pump Skimming Scam

The scammer sets-up a skimmer (credit card reader), which is usually impossible to detect, at a gas station pump. Here are some tips: (1) use a gas pump that is the most visible to the gas station attendant; (2) pay the attendant at the inside kiosk; and (3) review your credit card statements for unusual activity. Report any unusual activity to your credit card issuer immediately.

Grandparent Scam

Version # 1: The scammer will call the grandparent and claim that they are a grandchild. They are in trouble and need money, but don't want their parents to know, so they ask grandma/grandpa to wire some money to them.

Version # 2: The scammer will call the grandparent and claim that they are some authority figure (e.g., the Police) and that their grandchild has been arrested or was in a bad accident while on vacation, but the grandchild doesn't want his or her parents to know. Moreover, they state that the grandchild is in need of (or is asking for) money and is requesting the grandparent send it through wire transfer. Scammers may obtain information (e.g., name, location) about your grandchild on the internet, so don't assume, for instance, that the call is from the Royal Canadian Mounted Police (RCMP) because they know your grandson John is on vacation in Vancouver.

Here are some tips: (1) don't wire money unless you have verified the recipient's identity; (2) don't give the caller any information. If they state, "Your granddaughter has been arrested," then ask, "Who?" don't ask, "Jenny?" for example; (3) take down the caller's name, number, location, and organization. Verify the information independently; and (4) call the grandchild the caller referenced, or your other family to see if your grandchild is indeed out of town and, if so, whether they need assistance.

Home Improvement Scam

Version # 1: The scammer knocks on your door. When you answer he tells you that there is an issue with your roof, landscaping (e.g., a tree), or some other part of the house that needs "immediate repair." You step out with him to see what the issue is, leaving your door unlocked. An accomplice of the scammer then walks in the house and steals your property (wallet, purse, or other belongings).

Version # 2: The scammer knocks on your door. When you answer he tells you that there is an issue with your roof, landscaping (e.g., a tree), or some other part of the house that needs "immediate repair." He agrees to do the work to fix the issue immediately. You pay him in cash. The work is not done, unnecessary, or substandard.

Here are some tips: (1) don't answer the door if you weren't expecting someone and don't feel safe. Ask them through the door to leave a business card/other information about their business in the mailbox or under the door or, if they have no business card/other information, to leave your property. Report any suspicious activity to the police; (2) take some time to check out a contractor through the Better Business Bureau (BBB) and verify that they have a physical address, license, and are insured. Ask your neighbors or friends for references; (3) get a written contract, particularly if the cost is over $500; and (4) pay in increments and only make the final payment when you have verified that the work was done properly. Pay by credit card if possible. Alternatively, pay by check. Avoid paying cash.

Internet Scam (Nigerian Scam, Phishing, Ransomware, Scareware, and Mobile Pickpocketing)

The only way to stay 100% safe on the internet is not to use the internet. Scammers are attracted to the internet because they can reach thousands of consumers (potential victims) inexpensively and quickly; they can remain anonymous; and they have to deal with few internet restrictions, making it easy to place deceptive or misleading information online and/or create professional looking websites.

Nigerian or "419" Scam: The scammer sends out a mass email to many people, although it looks like you're the only one that's received it, hoping someone will take a bite. He typically alleges in the email that he is a lawyer who represents a deposed leader of a certain country (usually Nigeria) who has a large amount of money in the country, but needs your help to get it. Eventually you will be asked for your bank account number and/or money, to be used in order to bribe current government officials or to be used to pay fees before the money can be released. This was the first internet-age mass email scam. ("419" refers to the Nigerian criminal code regarding fraud.)

Phishing: The scammer (computer hacker) may attempt to obtain your personal information (computer username and password, credit card number, other financial information) by sending you an email or text message that looks like it's from a legitimate establishment (e.g., your bank, your utility company, Facebook, Twitter, Amazon, Google, DHL, FedEx, USPS), but it is not. Clicking on the attachment could infect your computer with malicious software ("malware"). Clicking on the link will bring you to a fake webpage. Any information you enter (e.g., username, password, credit card number) is captured by the hacker who controls the fake webpage. The hacker will either use this information to purchase goods or sell the information to other unscrupulous people.

Ransomware: The scammer (computer hacker) infects your computer with malicious software ("malware"), which makes an official-looking pop-up screen appear on your computer. Your computer is now frozen and the pop-up screen, which looks like it comes from the Federal Bureau of Investigation (FBI) or some other investigative agency of a national government, warns you that you have violated the law and that to unfreeze the computer you have to pay a fine.

Scareware: The scammer (computer hacker) infects your computer with malicious software ("malware"), which makes a pop-up screen appear on your computer warning you that a computer virus is infecting your computer. They, of course, offer anti-virus software that you need to pay for.

Mobile Pickpocketing: The scammer creates smartphone applications ("apps") or text messages that surreptitiously charge fees to smartphone users when they use the app or click on the link in the text message, by either hiding or not including terms of service by means of malicious software ("malware").

Here are some tips: (1) never click on an embedded link or open an attachment from an unsolicited or unexpected email or text message. If you can't verify the identity of the sender, then delete it without opening it. Independently go directly to the website you know by entering the secure address in the web browser and enter your login and password on the secure page. The internet address will start with "https" and an icon will be located to the right resembling a closed lock. Standard or nonsecure sites start with http. This stands for hypertext transfer (or transport) protocol and is the way the internet transfers data. The "s" in https means secure; (2) download any software or mobile device applications (or "apps") from reputable sources; (3) keep any of your application software up-to-date or remove it from your device. Third-party products such as Secunia or eEye Digital Security can quickly survey installed software and determine which need patches or updates; (4) use a complex password on your devices and service accounts. Consider using a passphrase. Weak passwords, such as "123456" or "password," or default passwords, will make your systems vulnerable. Also, use a different password for each of the services you use on the Web. And change your passwords periodically; (5) make sure your device is installed with a comprehensive security suite with anti-virus, anti-phishing, and firewall capabilities. Keep these up-to-date; (6) when working in a wireless hotspot offered by coffee shops, hotels, or airports, then limit your activity to web browsing only. Avoid using banking websites or going to service accounts requiring a password; (7) set social media sites to "Friends Only" or "Private"; (8) avoid setting "out-of-office" messages on personal email accounts, as this can confirm to spammers that your email address is legitimate and can provide information to unknown parties about your activities; (9) don't pay ransomware demands. Shutdown your computer and bring it to a computer technician for virus removal; (10) don't click on or download scareware. Use your existing anti-virus software to scan for viruses; and (11) avoid sending personal information through email or instant messaging.

Jury Duty Scam

The scammer, posing as a court officer or some other official, claims that you missed jury duty. In order to avoid criminal or other consequences for failing to show, they ask you to pay a penalty or fine. If you missed jury duty, then you would typically receive a notice in the mail, not a telephone call. If you do receive this call, take down all relevant information – caller's name, position, telephone number, the court he's calling from, etc. and independently verify the information. Do the same with any written letter you receive.

Medicare Scam

The scammer, who may work for a "Medicare mill," offers substandard or unneeded drugs, medical equipment, or other treatments. He may misrepresent the quantity of supplies actually provided or water down medications. The scammer may offer no treatment, medical supplies, or equipment at all, but, nonetheless, bill Medicare. Finally, the scammer may falsely diagnose a patient and subject them to unnecessary surgery.

This is what you can do (before the scam): (1) secure your Medicare card by keeping it in a safe place; (2) beware of "health fairs" with offers of "free screening." If it's indeed free, then they shouldn't be asking for your Medicare card; (3) keep records of doctor visits, tests, and procedures in a personal health care journal; (4) medicare doesn't call you or visit you to sell you anything; (5) thoroughly review your Medicare statements (Summary Notice and Part D Explanation of Benefits). Look for charges for treatment, drugs, or equipment you didn't get or items you were billed for more times than you received; and (6) talk to your medical provider when you don't understand the items you were billed for.

This is what you can do (after the scam): report suspected Medicare fraud here: http://www.stopmedicarefraud.gov/reportfraud/index.html or call 1-800-633-4227 or 1-800-447-8477.

Prescription Drug Scam

Scammers sell counterfeit or expired drugs over the

internet. Consumers have lots of choices for buying a prescription drug. But they need to beware when doing so because counterfeit drugs are on the rise. Not only do consumers risk throwing their money away on an ineffective drug, they could be harmed or killed by taking a drug that isn't what it seems to be. Marcia Bergeron died in 2006 after taking tainted pills bought over the internet. The medications she purchased came from a site that looked reputable, but were sent from overseas and contained high levels of lead, titanium, and arsenic.

This is what you can do (before the scam): (1) talk to your doctor before taking any prescription drugs; when you buy medications online, make sure the seller is located in the U.S. and is properly licensed and has a robust privacy policy. Check with your state board of pharmacy or the National Association of Boards of Pharmacy at www.nabp.net or call 1-847-391-4406. These sources can tell you if the online seller is licensed. Dealing with pharmacies that display the Verified Internet Pharmacy Practice Sites or VIPPS seal, or other similar certification seals, gives you more confidence that they and the products they sell are legitimate. A list of VIPPS-accredited pharmacies is located here: http://www.nabp.net/programs/accreditation/vipps/find-a-vipps-online-pharmacy/M(2); (2) make sure a licensed pharmacist is available to answer your questions. Whether you're buying prescription drugs online, through the mail, by telephone, or in person, reputable sellers should have pharmacists available to answer questions; (3) beware of online pharmacies that don't list an address or toll-free phone number to contact in case of a problem; (4) don't buy from an online seller that doesn't require a prescription; (5) don't buy from a site that advertises "miracle drugs" for a new cure for a serious disease. These drugs are not usually approved by the Food and Drug Administration (FDA) – a federal agency that protects public health – and could be ineffective or dangerous, posing risk to your health and well-being; and (6) avoid websites that only sell a limited number of medications, especially "lifestyle" medications that treat, for instance, obesity, impotence, or pain. Such websites are designed to attract consumers who have privacy concerns and wish to avoid an in-person doctor's visit. The websites are more likely to sell prescription drugs without legitimate prescriptions.

This is what you can do (after the scam): (1) if you believe that you have taken a counterfeit drug, then call 911 or your doctor for medical advice; (2) if you suspect you have bought a counterfeit drug online, report it. Notify the online drug seller. You should also report your suspicions about counterfeit drugs bought online to the FDA. Use the online reporting form located here: https://www.accessdata.fda.gov/scripts/medwatch/ or call the FDA's Medwatch program at 1-800-332-1088; and (3) if you believe an online drug seller is selling a prescription drug without a license, without a prescription, or in violation of other laws, report it. Use the FDA's online reporting form or call the FDA's Medwatch (see above for link or phone number). You should also report a suspicious site to your local state board of pharmacy, or the National Association of Boards of Pharmacy using their "Report a Suspicious Internet Pharmacy Site form," which is located here: http://www.nabp.net/programs/accreditation/vipps/report-a-site

Reloading Scam (a.k.a Refund or Recovery Scam or "Rip and Tear Scheme")

The scammer knows that the senior has been defrauded, either because they buy a "list of defrauded victims" or the scammer's colleague was the one who defrauded the victim, so they call stating that they are an authority (e.g., Police, FBI, law firm) and that they can get their money back. The victim is asked to pay a fee for their non-existent or substandard services.

These are some of the things you can do to avoid this fraud: (1) don't believe anyone who calls offering to recover money, merchandise, or prizes you never received, if the caller says you have to pay a fee in advance; (2) if someone claims to represent a government agency that will recover your lost money, merchandise, or prizes for a fee or a donation to a charity, then don't believe them, as the government doesn't operate in this manner. Report them immediately to the Federal Trade Commission. They may be contacted here: 1-877-FTC-HELP (1-877-382-4357). Legitimate federal, state, and local consumer protection agencies and nonprofit organizations do not charge for their services; (3) seek free available services, i.e., local Police, district attorney, friend first; and (4) if you are considering legal action, then select and consult with a trustworthy and reputable lawyer. Get references and check the Better Business Bureau and consumer agencies for any complaints.

What other frauds may the elder be subject to? The senior may be subject to being defrauded by a relative or caregiver. According to the National Center on Elder Abuse (http://www.ncea.aoa.gov/), in almost 90% of the elder abuse and neglect incidents where there was a known offender, the offender was a family member, and two-thirds of the offenders were adult children or spouses.

<u>Theft By Family Member</u>

The family member takes advantage of the elder's physical or mental condition to take property or money directly or indirectly by fraud or deception. These are the signs that make a senior susceptible: (1) their deceased spouse may have taken care of finances, so the surviving senior is now unfamiliar with how things work; (2) they don't understand new technology, such as online financial accounts and the online transfer of money; (3) they are not fluent in English; and (4) they are physically or mentally impaired.

These are the signs that someone is being financially abused: (1) their belongings, such as property, legal documents (e.g., will, title to the house), financial documents, personal identification or credit cards are missing; (2) financial statements are no longer coming to the elder's home; (3) changes in spending habits, such as buying items the elder doesn't need; (4) unusual withdrawals or other financial transactions on the bank or other financial accounts; (5) suspicious signatures on checks or other financial documents; (6) unpaid bills or shut-off notices for utilities or other services; (7) senior provides explanations about their finances that just don't make sense; (8) family member expresses excessive and unwarranted concern about how much money is being spent on the senior; (9) care being provided to the senior is not commensurate with his/her financial status; and (10) senior has an unkempt appearance (disheveled, soiled/ragged clothes, body odor).

These are the steps that you can take to protect the senior's assets: (1) encourage the senior, while they are cognitively well, to consult a trusted and reputable attorney or financial advisor (one of their choosing who they are comfortable with) before transferring property or giving large sums of money to anyone (including you); (2) encourage the senior to make a durable power of attorney, a legal document that states who they want to handle their finances, if they are unable to handle them. They can hire an attorney to draw up the papers for them or you can find the form online for free, but it's a good idea for the senior to have an attorney review the document before they sign it; (3) if they already have a durable power of attorney, but you feel that they were coerced into signing it or if you feel the person they named to handle their finances is mishandling them, you should both consult an attorney to find out how to go to court and ask a judge to appoint a different durable power of attorney; (4) if you are helping the senior with finances, keep them as involved as you can, depending on their physical or mental state; (5) encourage the senior to have their Social Security or other checks directly deposited into their bank account, in order to avoid unendorsed checks or cash lying around the house; (6) suggest that they secure valuables and important legal documents in a safe deposit box; and (7) notify the authorities if you believe your loved one has been a victim of elder financial abuse (or any other sort of abuse). Notify the police if someone has stolen money or property from your loved one. Notify Adult Protective Services if you believe they are being taken advantage of. To locate Adult Protective Services for a particular area call 1-800-677-1116.

Theft By Paid Caregiver

The caregiver takes advantage of the elder's physical or mental condition to take property or money directly or indirectly by fraud or deception. (For steps to take, see "Theft By Family Member" above.)

These are additional steps that you can take to protect the senior's assets: (1) deal with a reputable placement agency or company, one that does a thorough background check on the caregiver. Make sure the agency or company is bonded. Check them out with the Better Business Bureau and other consumer agencies; (2) consider doing your own background check on the caregiver; (3) don't give the caregiver access to the senior's valuables (e.g., jewelry), financial documents, legal documents (e.g., will, title to the house), or personal identification or credit cards; (4) don't allow the caregiver to deal with the elder's finances (e.g., going to the bank or doing bank transactions, balancing their checkbook, paying bills); (5) don't leave incoming/outgoing mail in an unsecured mailbox; (6) consider getting a shredder to destroy personal financial information; and (7) if you believe your loved one is being taken advantage of by a caregiver, then speak with the senior away from the caregiver to see how they are doing. Also, contact Adult Protective Services in your area. To locate Adult Protective Services in your area, call 1-800-677-1116.

Identity Theft

The scammer (identity thief) attempts to obtain your personal information, e.g., social security number, bank account number, credit card number, ATM card and PIN number, in order to sell it or assume your identity and use it themselves. This may be the crime we need to be most concerned about in the future. It leaves victims in a quandary, as they need to prove their innocence. Identity theft wasn't recognized as a specific federal offense until Congress passed the Identity Theft and Assumption Deterrence Act in 1998.

These are the things you can do (before you are a victim of identity theft): (1) protect yourself from identity theft by protecting your personal information. Never give personal information (whether banking account number, credit card number, or social security number) to someone who has made unsolicited contact with you. Only give personal information to people/institutions that you know are legitimate; (2) don't give more than the last four digits of your social security number to a financial institution's telephone representative; (3) invest in a shredder. Shred any personal financial or private documents you no longer need, e.g., old bank or financial statements, Medicare statements, doctor bills, before throwing them away; (4) cover the input screen with your other hand whenever entering your PIN number or zip code; (5) have your paycheck and other checks directly deposited into your bank account; (6) keep your social security card and Medicare card secure; don't carry them in your wallet or purse on a daily basis; (7) keep your financial documents and other personal documents secure; and (8) obtain credit reports at least yearly and review them. If there are transactions on your account that you are not familiar with, then it could mean that you are a victim of identity theft or there is an error on your credit report. If there is an error, then initiate a dispute with the credit reporting agency showing the error. All credit rating agencies must provide you with a free credit report once annually. These agencies are as follows: Experian – https://www.experian.com or 1-888-397-3742; TransUnion – https://www.disclosure.transunion.com or 1-800-888-4213; Equifax – https://www.equifax.xom/home/en_us or 1-800-685-1111; and Innovis – https://www.innovis.com/InnovisWeb/ or 1-800-540-2505.

These are the things you can do (after you are a victim of identity theft): (1) create an "Identity Theft Report" here: https://www.consumer.ftc.gov/articles/0277-create-identity-theft-report or call the Federal Trade Commission at 1-877-438-4338; (2) immediately report the fraud to your credit card companies, bank, and other financial services firms that you use; (3) immediately have one of the credit reporting agencies place a fraud alert on your credit report, which will make it harder for the identity thief to open more accounts in your name. The alert last 90 days, but you may renew it; and (4) order credit reports periodically.

PART III

The Underlying Psychological Facilitators

The story presented in Chapter 12 ("By Jove, You Were Right!) and Chapter 13 ("Like Taking Candy From a Baby") is fictitious. The names of the individuals, and companies, except for Apple Computer, are also fictitious. No identification with actual persons, living or deceased, or companies, except for Apple Computer, should be inferred.

CHAPTER 12
By Jove, You Were Right!

January 25th

Mary sat on her sofa and waited for justice. That was being meted out by that stern, no-nonsense *Judge Judy*, as Mary watched her favorite TV program. The phone rang while she watched, but she didn't quite ignore it, thinking, "Who could that be?" And, each time it rang, Skittles would look up in bewilderment, its eyes peeled and focused on the direction of the ring, and apparently wondering, "What's that?!" Skittles was Mary's American Shorthair cat. Then a commercial came on – something about toilet paper, and the phone rang again. Mary answered it. "Hello," she said. A voice on the other end said, "Hello, Mrs. Warren?" Mary cleared her throat. "Yes, this is Mrs. Warren, what can I help you with?" she asked, while thinking, "I hope this isn't another charity. I already gave enough to the American Heart Association last month." Mary was a big supporter of the AHA. Her husband, James, had died of a heart attack five years ago, and she now felt obliged to help in the fight against heart disease. She also gave money to her church. It wasn't the same, taking that walk to the 10 a.m. Sunday service without Roger. "This is James D. Smith from Big Fortune Financial, and I have a great opportunity for you," the caller said. Mary was shaken out of her deep wistful thoughts. "Uh. Well, uh, James, I already do my banking at One USA Bank, and most of my money is tied up in CDs," Mary said. "Please call me James. I'm not calling from a bank, but a stock brokerage that I'm the president of. It's a great day here in Palm Springs. Isn't it?" Smith asked. As he spoke, Mary couldn't help thinking that the caller had the same name as her late husband. He didn't even wait for her to respond, and continued without taking a breath.

"I have this great stock that's guaranteed to go up. It's called Apple Computer. You've surely heard of that. No?" Mary had heard of Apple. She'd seen its commercials plenty of times, and saw how attached her grandchildren were to their iPhones. "Why, yes. Of course I'm familiar with Apple, but I'm invested in CDs and I'd like to stay…" Before she could go on, she was interrupted by Smith. "Listen, Mrs. Warren," he said, "What could you be making in those CDs? Less than one percent, I'm sure. This is a great opportunity that you're going to miss. We just put our best clients in it today." Mary said, "I'm going to be paying for some of my grandchildren's college and, before I do, I need to be sure it's in a safe investment like CDs. Stocks seem too risky." Mary then glanced down as Skittles rubbed her leg. "We carefully research all our recommendations," said Smith, "and we're certain they'll do well. I'll tell you what we do. I'll let you see how this stock does in a week. If it does well, I'll call you back, and we'll do some business. How does that sound?" Mary thought for a moment, and then glanced at the TV. "Sure," she said, and thought, "Although he's polite, I hope I won't have to hear from him again." Smith said, "Mrs. Warren. Thank you for your time. We'll speak next week. I'm looking forward to it." Mary took a quick glance at the TV again, and then looked down at Skittles. "But…," she said. Smith had already hung up. After a few beats, she thought, "Darn, I missed the second half of *Judge Judy*."

February 1st

As Mary sat at her kitchen table going through the mail – and she'd receive quite a pile each day, James from Big Fortune Financial was the last thing on her mind when the phone rang. It didn't take long for Skittles' ears to perk up when it did. "Hello," Mary answered. "Hello, Mrs. Warren. It's James. You remember me, the president of Big Fortune Financial. Have you seen Apple?" The stock went nuts! It's up over 15% since we spoke!"

Mary had to get her bearings, as she wasn't expecting this call. "Hi, James. I don't know if I want to invest in stocks. I'm invested in CDs," she said. "Mrs. Warren, we had an agreement! When we last spoke you agreed to do business with me, if I could show you the stock made money! Now you're reneging on that! Is that how you were raised?! You should show a little more respect, especially to someone who is trying to help you and your family!" Mary was taken aback. "I'm sorry. You said the stock's done well?" she asked. "Yes. It's up over 15% in just five trading days. Not bad, uh?! A lot better than your CDs. By the way, when's the last time your banker called you about those CDs?! Mrs. Warren, let's take a look at how it's done. Listen, are you near a computer?" Smith asked. Mary had a desktop computer that she'd keep on a desk in her kitchen. She used it mostly to pay her bills and email her daughter, son-in-law, and grandchildren, all of whom lived in Phoenix, Arizona. Sometimes she'd use it to play a free roulette game on the internet. "Yes. It's already turned on. What do you need me to do?" she asked. "Okay, we're going to go to Yahoo Finance, just type that in your search engine," said Smith. "Okay, I think I know how to get there. My husband, James, and I owned some dividend stocks before. I only sold them after he died," she said. Smith said, "I'm sorry to hear that Mrs. Warren. My father died just six months ago, and it still pains me today. How old was your husband when he passed?" Mary had tears in her eyes. "He was 67. He had just retired when he had a heart attack," she said. "Oh, I'm so sorry, Mrs. Warren," he said. "You can call me Mary. What would you like me to type into Yahoo Finance, James?" she asked. He said, "Okay, Mary, go to the Quote Lookup and type A-A-P-L. That's the stock symbol for Apple Computer. You can see it's up just a little over 15% since we last spoke." Mary looked at Apple's stock chart on Yahoo Finance and said, "By Jove, you were right!" Smith then continued, "But, listen, you missed that opportunity. Don't get me wrong. I still think it's a great opportunity, but you missed the 15% rise. There's another stock that I'd like to talk to you about that's going to rise even more. It's Nettor Pharmaceutical Group. They have a leukemia drug in the pipeline that's going to be approved by the FDA. And nobody knows that news yet, but it's going to come out soon. You've got to get into this stock before they announce. It's trading at $8.50. Besides the fact it's going to take off big time, it's a company that's near and dear to my heart. My younger sister died of leukemia when I was 10." Mary thought how unfortunate it was that James D. Smith's sister had died at such a young age and terrible disease. "Oh, I'm so sorry," Mary said, "You know maybe it wouldn't be such a bad idea to buy 100 shares." Smith said, "Now Mary, this is the opportunity of a lifetime. I'm putting my best clients in it, and hope to put some new clients, like you, in it too. Now, you're telling me you only have $850 in CDs?! Think of what you'll be able to do with the gains from this stock. You'll be able to take care of your grandkids with the money you're going to make. You can pay for their education like you planned. And the cost of education these days, it's a wonder anyone can afford it, right?! Listen, Mary, the minimum share quantity we usually require is 20,000 shares...." Mary was so taken aback that the telephone receiver slightly left her ear. "That seems like a lot," Mary said. Smith continued, "But, I'm going to do you a favor. As the president of Big Fortune Financial, I'll cut that in half – to 10,000 shares. You surely have at least $85,000 in your CDs." Mary looked around the corner of her kitchen to see if she could see Skittles. "I don't know, Mary said. "That's an awful lot of money." Smith replied, "Mary, I showed you how I made money in Apple Computer, and you promised to do business with me if I did. Now, I'm going to make money for you in Nettor Pharma. It's guaranteed to make money." Mary relented. "Okay, seeing as it's developing worthwhile medicines, I can do 10,000 shares, but no more." He said, "Excellent. You've made a great decision. I'm going to email you some forms to complete, and I need you to wire the money to Big Fortune Financial. I'll give you instructions in an email. We need to do this quick, and you need to keep mum about it, because the news isn't out yet about Nettor's leukemia cancer drug approval. You won't regret doing business with me Mary. Do you understand the steps?" "Yes," Mary replied, "I understand." Mary peered around the corner of her kitchen again in search of Skittles. "Okay, great. Can you get to the bank today to get this money to me so I can make the purchase for you?" Smith asked. "Okay. Yes. I'll do it this morning," Mary said. "Great. As soon as we receive the money, we'll make the purchase, and you'll be on your way to making a fortune. Thanks Mary," said Smith. "Thank you James," said Mary, as her head continued to bob as she wondered, "Where's Skittles?" She slowly hung up the receiver, and called out, "Skiiiittlllles…"

February 29ᵗʰ

Mary had awoken on a Monday morning and went through her usual routine. She'd read the Bible aloud to herself, and incidentally to Skittles, who sat on Mary's lap, as Mary sat on her La-Z-Boy recliner in the living room. On this morning, she was turned to the Book of Matthew in the New Testament. She started reading from where she left off yesterday.

After about forty minutes she was done reading, so she placed the Bible on the end table, and then walked into the kitchen for breakfast. Mary poured some dry cat food into Skittles's fish-designed bowl. As she prepared her own meal, however, she started to feel anxious. She stopped what she was doing and took a deep breath, turned on her computer, and logged in, determined to see what was happening with Nettor Pharmaceutical. "I haven't heard from James. Have they released the big news?" she thought. She was going to find out for herself, as the last few weeks seemed liked a lifetime, and she couldn't wait any longer. As she typed N-E-T-P into Yahoo Finance's symbol lookup box she was filled with anxiety. Then the price came back. It was "0.0001." Suddenly, her face became flush, her heart had a couple of erratic beats, and her whole body was tense. "Am I reading this correctly?"she asked herself. Mary went into Yahoo Finance's "News" section, but there wasn't any recent news for N-E-T-P. "It can't be, it just can't be," she said. She decided to type "Nettor Pharmaceutical" into Google to see if there was more information. The first hit was a PDF document on the Securities and Exchange

Commission's website. She had some vague understanding of the SEC. She knew it was part of the federal government and it was established to protect investors. She opened the PDF and started to read it to herself sotto voce. "It appears to the Securities and Exchange Commission that the public interest and the protection of investors require a suspension of trading in the securities of Nettor Pharmaceutical Group (NETP) because of concerns regarding the accuracy and adequacy of information in the marketplace and potentially manipulative transactions in NETP's common stock." She then asked herself, "What does this mean? What's happened to my investment? Mary continued, "There must be some mistake. No. I know how to read this. I need to call James." She went to her email to get his number and phoned him. No one answered. After five rings, a recorded voice said, "Your call has been forwarded to an automated voice messaging system…" As Mary listened, she thought, "I shouldn't have bought this stock." Mary was shaking. After the beep, she said, "This is Mary Warren. I'm calling for James D. Smith. Please have him call Mary Warren. That's W-a-r-r-e-n," Mary said. "James has sold me a stock. Nettor Pharmaceutical. It's trading at what seems like zero, and he sold it to me at $8.50 just a few weeks ago. This can't be right. Please call me back!"

A few hours later, the phone rang. Mary answered. "Good morning, Mrs. Warren. It's James and I know why you're calling. I can't tell you how disappointed I am in Nettor. I had a lot of faith in this company, and its leukemia drug. They had me fooled. I've also lost a lot of money," said Smith. "Where's my money?!," Mary asked. Smith replied, "That's just it Mary. The stock's essentially at zero. Our investments have been wiped out. I know how you feel. I feel the same way. But, we can't let this setback get us down. You're a tough lady Mary. I know that. And I know I need to make it up to you." Mary mouth was agape for a few seconds before she started speaking as loud as thunder. "I've lost it all?! How could this happen?! This was my retirement money!," Mary said. She then broke down and cried. Mary composed herself after a few moments and then asked, "How could this have happened? I needed that money." She then fell into a silent shock. "Mary I can't tell you how badly I feel. You're a tough lady and we can bounce back together. Please let me make this loss up to you. I know I can. Now I know Nettor Pharma let us down, but let's talk about another company whose owner I know personally. It's Torten Energy Group. Its symbol is O-I-L-Y…"

CHAPTER 13
Like Taking Candy From a Baby

January 25th

Jake Moore sat on the side of an old mahogany desk and waited for the roomful of sales agents to settle down. "Listen up, guys! You know what we're pushing today. Nettor Pharma. We've gotta get this baby past $5. You've got your scripts. Do what you need to do to sell it." One of those agents – Greg Sommers, a muscle bound five-foot-three-inch 45-year-old who liked his suits tight and ties long, was raring to go. He started his day lifting weights at Sona's Gym, working his chest, shoulders, and triceps. He then had breakfast – four raw eggs and a power bar, before arriving at work just before 8:30. At 9 he'd spend the next eight hours dialing for dollars. "When is this guy gonna shut up?" Greg thought. "We're increasing your take on this," Moore continued. "Instead of 15%, where doubling it to 30%. The room erupted in excited hoots and jubilant hollers, as the agents' incentives just doubled. "So hit those phones, guys." Greg thought, "Yeah, hit the burner phones. Burn-her. Ha, ha, ha. Burn-her." Without much of a pause, the room became a boisterous cacophony, filled with animal spirits, with whiffs of sweat on their trail.

Greg, without so much as a pause, picked up his smartphone and started making his cold calls. First on what he liked to call his "hit list" was Peggy Willens. He knew she was a divorced 66 year old who lived in Naples, Florida. "I'd like to be in sunny Florida right about now," he thought. "I'm calling from the Big Apple, but she'll see I'm calling from the 239 area code. Naples. I love this burner app. Aah, the beauty of technology. It's probably sunny, but I better check the weather down there." As he searched online on his laptop, he dialed Peggy. "Hi. Peggy Willens?" Greg asked, and, after a slight pause he said, "Listen

Peggy, I'm James D. Smith. Please call me James. I'm calling from a stock brokerage that I'm the president of, and I have a great opportunity for you. It's a great day here in Naples. Isn't it?" and before she could answer, he continued, "I have this stock that's guaranteed to go down. It's called Apple Computer. You've surely heard of that. No? Anyway, we can profit from that by selling the stock short or purchasing some puts. Yeah, let me tell you how that works. If the stock goes down, you'll make money. We just told our best clients about this opportunity today, and we want to make it available to a few other select people." After some back and forth, Smith said, "I'll tell you what we do. I'll let you see how this stock does in a week. If it goes down, I'll call you back, and we'll do some business. Sound like a plan?" For four hours, Greg would make calls to over 100 people, mostly elderly woman living alone, and he'd tell them he expected Apple Computer to trade lower. He'd then spend the "second half," as he'd like to call the next four hours after the first four, telling prospects he was certain Apple Computer or A-A-P-L was going to move higher. Either way, it was a foolproof plan. As long as he picked a volatile stock, and Apple lately had been more volatile than a teenager's mood swings, it was bound to have a significant move, either up or down, particularly with an earnings announcement coming soon. He didn't care in which direction it moved, as long as it moved. A week from now, about half the people he called would think that Greg, or "James", as they knew him, was a stock market genius.

February 1st

The mass of steel that was Greg Sommers, walking as if he owned the sidewalk, made a quick left and entered a non-descript building in one of the grittiest, rundown parts of New York City. "I wonder what they're leasing this piece of s____ office for?" he thought to himself. Earlier this morning, he worked out his back, biceps, and abs. As he walked up the two flights and entered the office, he ran into Jake Moore. "Hiya Jake. This is going to be a great day. Whoever said 'don't pitch the b_____' sure got it wrong. Well, maybe they were right about the young ones, but not the old bags, and today, I'm going to prove it." Jake said, "N-E-T-P's starting to move. We need some more wind behind its sails." Greg thought, "I don't need this guy's advice" and said, "No problem, Jake. It'll be higher by the end of today. Did you take a look at Apple. It's up over 15% this past week. Half the people I called last week, I'm gonna call back today and they're gonna think I'm the greatest investor since Warren Buffett." Jake laughed. But Greg only smirked, relishing his cleverness.

Greg, as "James," hit the phones at 9 sharp, and the morning and first part of the afternoon flew by. It was now 1 p.m. and Greg had already sold over half a million shares of Nettor, as the stock moved from $2.75 to $8.00, to his "clients." Greg thought to himself, "I need to start calling those old moochers on the West Coast." He started with Joanne Winkler, who bought 20,000 shares of N-E-T-P. "She's a big fish," Greg thought. Then he moved on to Mary Warren. "Hello, Mrs. Warren. It's James. You remember me..."

After his successful close of Warren, he moved on to Susan Myers, then Roberta Gomez, and Trina Jones. Greg moved over two million shares of Nettor Pharma stock. He was right. It was a great day – for Big Fortune Financial, for the other sales agents, and for him. "These old women are such SAPs – Sad and Pathetic. It's like taking candy from a baby," he thought. "Am I the greatest salesman, or what?!"

Over the next few days, Greg's sales job with regard to N-E-T-P was over. He knew that his "clients" were buying big chunks of stock, driving the price higher and higher, while those behind Nettor Pharma – the stock promoters, and other insiders, were dumping their stock, obtained at very low prices, into the rise. Greg was looking forward to the long three day weekend and had plans to fly down to Miami Beach and spend some of the loot he had earned from touting Nettor. He was going to leave on his trip with the assurance that he was raking it in, and would continue to do so.

February 29th

Jake paced the sales floor of Big Fortune Financial. "Guys, great job on Nettor Pharma. We got our backers out before the stock tanked. But now we've got a new stock to push. It's Torten Energy. It's symbol is O-I-L-Y and we need to turn this baby into a gusher." Greg thought, "What an idiot," as Jake continued, "Work the same suckers you put into Nettor. I know. You're thinking, 'These people are sitting on losses. Why would they buy from me?' Well, people hate losses, so tell 'em you'll make it up to them. They're probably good for one more round. The best people to pitch are the ones in this very situation. Get it done." Greg, having done an early morning workout of his hamstrings, quads, and calves, was as confident, determined, and ready to sell as he's ever been. As he perused his "sucker list" on his desktop computer screen, he thought, "Which old lady's ass am I gonna kick first?" Then his phone rang. He looked at his "hit list" and saw that it was Mary Warren.

CHAPTER 14
Fade to Black

That's all Folks! You probably want to know what's happened to Mary Warren. Did she call the authorities? Did she get her money back? Did she continue "investing" with "James D. Smith," perhaps buying O-I-L-Y? You might also want to know what's happened with Greg Sommers (alias, James D. Smith). Is he still scamming older women? Was he ever arrested? You can write your own ending. While the story presented in "By Jove, You Were Right!" and "Like Taking Candy From a Baby" is fictitious, the fact is that some of these situations turn out with a happy ending, and others don't. We, as fraud fighters, want to strive for the best result, which is getting seniors to avoid these situations. After all, an ounce of prevention is worth a pound of cure.

What do we know about Mary? We know she is decent and religious. She keeps her commitments, and may have felt compelled by her faithfulness to this personal characteristic to invest. Mary is also lonely, and maybe she looked forward to speaking to somebody, anybody, even "James D. Smith." Sometimes our religious convictions present us with a struggle. Can we be kind, while also standing up for ourselves?

What do we know about Greg Sommers? We know he is self-centered, and only cares about lining his own pocket. Greg will use all the manipulative techniques at his disposal to achieve his goals. Some of these methods included making people feel guilty for not keeping their commitments; getting people to like him by pointing out commonalities, whether true or not; getting prospects to believe that there is something that's exclusive and non-public about what he's offering; and convincing people that he's in an authoritative role.

No professional financial advisor will call you out of the blue and start touting a stock. They'll want to meet you in person, and get to know your financial situation, your tolerance for risk, and what your financial goals are. You, in turn, should get to know them, and compare them to others, ultimately selecting someone you are comfortable with.

Situations like the one presented in "By Jove, You Were Right!" and "Like Taking Candy From a Baby" have occurred, and continue to do so. According to a Ropes & Gray legal summary, Joseph R. Berkowitz, who is co-Chief of the SEC's Microcap Fraud Task Force, has identified a growing trend of stock fraud cases targeting senior citizens. Mr. Berkowitz expects this trend to continue.

In September 2016, the Securities and Exchange Commission, which is a Federal stock market and public company regulator, recently filed a complaint (*SEC v. Craig V. Sizer and Miguel Mesa*) against two individuals who defrauded 600 investors, many of whom were elderly and unsophisticated, out of $20 million. These two defendants were also charged criminally by the U.S. Attorney in Florida. The SEC alleges that they set-up and operated "boiler rooms" that used high-pressure and manipulative sales tactics to push the stock of companies in which they had a significant interest. According to the SEC's complaint, they told investors that they were raising money to fund a company's research and development, and that no sales commissions would be paid out from investor funds. It turns out that they misappropriated approximately ninety percent of the funds raised from investors, enriching themselves and paying sales commissions to the boiler-room agents. Neither their operation nor the sales agents were properly registered, according to the SEC's complaint.

CHAPTER 15
Criminal Minds

Those like the fictional fraudster, Greg Sommers, have gone by many names: Bamboozler, Bunco Artist, Cheater, Chiseler, Con Artist, Confidence Man, Criminal, Demon, Fleecer, Flim-Flam Man, Fraudster, Grafter, Grifter, Gypster, Hornswoggler, Huckster, Mammon, Scalawag, Schemer, Scammer, Smoothie, Snake Oil Salesman, Sharpie, Silver-Tongued Devil, Smoothie, Stealer, Swindler, Robber, and Thief.

We don't hang out with people like this, so we sometimes think they don't exist. They do. That's not to say we don't know there is evil in this world. We do. However, we just don't expect it to rear its ugly head on the other line of our phone, or at our door, or like Lena Jarrow, the victim of a "promissory note peddler," across from the dinner table. We're in a fog at the outset, and don't see the ugliness yet. Whatever we call them, they don't rob people with a gun, but use their wits and deception to get money from you. There is no evil the criminal won't stoop to. Ralph Waldo Emerson wrote that, "every violation of truth is not only a sort of suicide in the liar, but it is a stab at the health of human society." These criminals live with corrupt souls, and destroy human lives in a manner that can't possibly be measured.

The fraudsters out there don't come one-size-fits-all. Some are devoutly religious, or at least seem so, others are not. Some are well-educated, others are not. Some are rich, others are poor. Some are young, others are old. Some are men, others are women. You usually don't know the fraudster when you first see him because, at that point, he looks like just about anyone. One thing that they do have in common is that fraudsters attempt to make psychological connections with their victims, although they tend to be emotionally detached.

The adept fraudster displays Barnemesque attributes – a gift for gab, for theatrics, for putting on a show. He creates a fantasy world, and lures you in. As children we love to pretend and live in a fantasy world. Perhaps some of that never leaves us. Voltaire, the 18th century French philosopher, said, "Illusion is the first of all pleasure." You should be aware of this tendency, and try to get yourself into reality, where you'll be better able to discern if an investment, or other opportunity, is worthwhile. Fraudsters are artists at duping us – who paint the picture they want us to see, a picture that will change your behavior, and get you to do what they want. A criminal's ingenuity, when combined with his greed, is a powerful force. Fraudster's engage in nefarious conduct because they don't expect to get caught. There's no financial crime they won't commit, from the chain letter – the nickel and dime version of the Ponzi scheme – to more intricate investment frauds.

Let's take some time to get into the fraudster's mind. We need to understand him if we are to protect ourselves. Lines 7-12 of Canto 17 of Dante Alighieri's *The Inferno*, tells you everything you need to know about the fraudster:

> *And that uncleanly image of deceit*
>
> *Came up and thrust ashore its head and bust,*
>
> *But on the border did not drag its tail*
>
> *The face was as the face of a just man,*
>
> *Its semblance outwardly was so benign,*
>
> *And of the serpent all the trunk beside.*

If you are looking for a monster, then you won't find him in the fraudster at the time you are most vulnerable to fraud – at the outset, when you first meet him or her. At that time you'll see someone who is "benign," a kind, well-mannered, forthright, and respected male – most often, but a female too. They'll often be a well-dressed and trusted figure of someone with both authority and expertise ("a just man"). It's not until later, after you've been scammed, that you'll see the beast ("the serpent all the trunk beside"). Just like that your perception of the same individual will change. For example, even a nun, who we view as devoutly religious and righteous, can be both a victim and scammer. In 2009, William J. Boyle was barred from the securities industry for misappropriating his clients' funds. One of his clients was a 64-year old Catholic nun that had inherited $532,000 from her mother and, because the nun took a vow of poverty, she wanted the money to go to her religious order. That's a nun as victim. In 1997 Sister Susan Walsh, who was a stockbroker before becoming a nun, got involved in a scheme that conned investors. That's a nun as scammer.

When we look at, and assess, a person, our perception of what we see is skewed by our own biases. We tend to take mental shortcuts, known as "heuristics," in the technical jargon. We simplify our thinking, and become certain of it. For example, with the "representativeness heuristic," which leads one to focus on anecdotal social cues and markers when making judgments, when we see a nun, we aren't thinking scammer. We're thinking, this is a good and virtuous woman. If we're aware of these tendencies, then perhaps we can correct them.

According to Robert B. Cialdini, the author of *Influence*, individuals can utilize six tactics to get people to act. Some people use these tactics with no nefarious intent, but we know that fraudsters do operate with an evil mind. They use these methods to get what they want: your money. These tactics are like knives. You can use knives to do something constructive, like cut an apple, or something destructive, like kill someone. Fraudsters use these tactics deceptively in order to harm you. They want to kill your spirit and take your money. These methods are the means by which these criminals ply their dishonest and despicable trade.

The six tactics are authority, consistency, liking, reciprocation, scarcity, and social proof, described more fully below.

<u>Authority</u>: The scammer may lie and say, "I'm the president of this company," expecting the targeted victim to be honored and humbled to be speaking to the "president of the company." They may say, "This is Special Agent Smith from the FBI, and it looks like you've entered a website that you're prohibited from accessing under U.S. law." Other examples include: "I'm the Commissioner of Jurors, and you've missed jury duty"; "This is the Massachusetts State Police. Your grandson, Timmy, has been arrested"; "This is David Jones calling from Georgia Power. We see that you haven't paid your bill, and your power will, therefore, be cut off"; and "This is Pam Brown. I'm a Revenue Agent with the IRS."

People tend to yield, and listen, to authority. Perhaps you remember the actor Robert Young in the Sanka commercials. After Marcus Welby, MD, we always perceived him as a doctor, a medical authority, so why wouldn't we listen to him when he asked us to drink "coffee...without caffeine."

Fraudsters are confident and self-assured; they consider it essential that they wear accoutrements that exude status and wealth, in addition to having a fine car, home, and/or office. These are status symbols that create perceptions in your mind that might not be accurate. Get the facts first. In the investment context, verify they have the degrees, certifications, or licenses they claim to have. Focus on red flags, i.e., signals or information you can spot that will alert you to contradictions, inconsistencies, and implausibilities. Keep note of these. They might need you, not to invest with them necessarily, but as a reference, making you an unwitting accomplice in their fraud. Don't give references.

Consistency: Fraudsters try, by tenacity or trickery, to get people to make commitments. Once people do, then the scammer has got them in their trap. They know that it's difficult for people to renege on their commitments. People want to remain consistent. The fraudster may get someone to make a commitment by saying, "I know $100,000 may be a lot to invest in this venture. I normally don't do this for clients, but how about investing $50,000 and letting me earn your trust?" Once the recipient of this question provides their assent, the fraudster will let them know if they show any inkling of reneging on that.

People have a tendency to want to reduce "cognitive dissonance." This tendency is one of our biases that the fraudster may take advantage of. Let me explain. The American social psychologist, Leon Festinger, noted that we strive for consistency because when we experience inconsistency we become mentally uncomfortable. He called this uneasiness we feel "cognitive dissonance," and the fraudster may take advantage of this by pointing out even minor inconsistencies. The scammer, knowing that we want to reduce this discomfort, will try to highlight any inconsistencies we may make.

Professor Barry Staw is an authority on organizational behavior who teaches at Berkeley. In a research study he ran, Staw found that students studying for a Masters of Business Administration (MBA) degree, who you might appropriately think are financially astute when making investment decisions, actually maintained a losing deal even in the face of dire consequences, because once a commitment was made to the investment they didn't want to be inconsistent. The innate desire to fight "cognitive dissonance" is that strong!

Liking: The fraudster will try to make a connection with you, and will treat you respectfully, so you'll get to like him. This, of course, may be innocuous or it may be the fraudster's first step in getting his hands on your money. They may try to see you often, or as often as it takes. Familiarity breeds cooperation – your cooperation with the fraudster. Also, there's a lot of information about you online that the fraudster will use to tailor his pitch and get you to like him.

You tend to like people who bring you what may seem like good news ("you've won a prize") or expected investment profits ("my investment fund has earned around 10% consistently over the last few years, and your guaranteed to earn at least that much"), but what is in reality a fantasy. The fraudster in creating a fantasy, is attempting to disconnect you from reality and logical, critical thinking. He's brought you this fantasy and you like him for it.

The scammer will also compliment you, which makes you like them. Who doesn't like a compliment? Take Mark Twain, who said, "I can live two months on a good compliment," or Mae West's alluringly direct, "Flattery will get you everywhere."

Fraudsters are usually accomplished conversationalists. They try to create rapport with those they engage, while constantly trying to hunt for common links, whether those are religious, political, or sports-related, among others. While scammers try to make a human connection as do non-fraudsters, the difference is that scammers have a nefarious intent, while non-fraudsters don't have such an intent.

Reciprocation: The fraudster may say, "I haven't done this for other people, but I'm going to make an exception to the minimum investment amount that needed for you to invest with me." Looks like he's given you something, but will you feel the need to reciprocate? Most of the time we will feel that need, in quid pro quo fashion, and the fraudster knows it. Leonardo da Vinci said, "It is easier to resist in the beginning than at the end." Once you except anything from the fraudster, then you'll feel more of a need to reciprocate. This often happens with unscrupulous free lunch seminars. Most people will feel an obligation after attending one. Fight the urge to reciprocate and, if you can't, then don't accept. If you do, then judge the investment on its own merits, and the person recommending it on their own merits.

Scarcity: The fraudster may say, "This investment opportunity will be available for a limited time, and it's nearly fully subscribed to." You'll feel the need to jump in because you don't want to miss out. The more time you have to contemplate the investment, the more time you might do some deep thinking.

Social Proof: Many times the fraudster will use people as references to vouch for them. The reference, your friend or relative perhaps, might say, "I've made a great deal of money with this guy, so have others." You'll feel the need to get in on the action, so as not to be left out of this great opportunity. In such circumstances, it may be best for you to make like Groucho Marx, who said, "I don't want to belong to any club that would accept me as a member."

"Where all think alike, no one thinks very much," Walter Lippmann, the Cold-War-era political commentator, once said. Don't play this "monkey see, monkey do" game. Invest on the merits, not because those you know are putting in their money.

All six tactics are used effectively, and in short order, in the movie Boiler Room. A "boiler room" is a shady brokerage operation that features high-pressure sales tactics in order to sell low-priced, shady securities. And this movie, from 2000, is about a college dropout who gets a job as a broker at one of these boiler rooms.

<u>Authority and Liking</u>:

Chris Varick *("boiler room" stockbroker) Hi, Dr. Jacobs, this is Chris Marlin over at JT Marlin.*

Dr. Jacobs *(potential client who was telephoned) Marlin?*

Chris Varick *Right. He's my father....So my associate tells me you're interested in one of our stocks.*

Dr. Jacobs *Yes, MSC (the symbol of the stock Varick is pushing) sounds like it might be interesting.*

<u>Social Proof</u>:

Dr. Jacobs *Well, I still have to run it by my people.*

Chris Varick *That's great, Doc. If you want to miss yet another opportunity here and go watch your colleagues get rich doing clinical trials, then don't buy a share and hang up the phone.*

<u>Scarcity, Liking, Reciprocation, and Consistency</u>:

Chris Varick *Now, since you're a new account I cannot go any higher than two thousand shares. I'd love to but I just can't do it.*

Dr. Jacobs *Two thousand?! Whoa! That's way more than I was thinking about. Two thousand, Jesus. (pause) I'm just curious, why can't you sell me more than that?*

Chris Varick *Well, we like to establish a relationship with our clients on something small before we get to the more serious trades. Let me show you several percentage points on this small trade and then we'll talk about doing future business.*

Dr. Jacobs *That sounds good. Give me two thousand shares.*

Chris Varick *Done.*

Dr. Jacobs *You sure you can't do any better on this one?*

Chris Varick *No, I'm sorry, Dr. Jacobs.*

Dr. Jacobs *Alright, let's start with this trade then.*

Chris Varick *Great. I promise we'll go big on the next one.*

Another tactic that fraudsters use is control and intimidation or scare tactics, particularly when utilizing the phone to scam people. These criminals are attempting to arouse the emotion of fear in their victims. The victim doesn't want to feel the emotion of fear and, thus, tries to get rid of it. One common, and simple, way to do that is to acquiesce to the scammer's demands.

In their book *Weapons of Fraud*, Anthony Pratkanis and Doug Shadel discuss "The Undercover Taping Project." This project dealt with law enforcement obtaining undercover audiotapes of real scammers believing they were calling seniors who had been scammed multiple times, but were, in fact, calling criminal investigators posing as those seniors. The excerpted and edited dialogue presented below, entitled "The Free Prize Pitch" by Pratkanis and Shadel, is based on one of those calls.

Robert Banks *(Scammer) You'll remember that we had told you earlier in the year that because of your past failings and disappointments we were going to put you in for a final cash award. And should you be contacted on it, that it would mean anywhere from 10,000 to a quarter of a million dollars for you. You don't have a quarter of a million coming, but you did better than ten grand. Do you think that Tuesday afternoon you could use a $50,000 cashier's checks to straighten something up?*

Darlene Parker *(Investigator posing as a victim) What does it cost me?*

Robert Banks *OK, that's all you have to say, ma'am?*

Darlene Parker *Yes.*

Robert Banks *You know something, boy, ma'am, would you like your award. It's $50,000. Do you want it? Yes or no?*

Darlene Parker *Of course.*

Robert Banks *OK. Then here's my suggestion to you, Ok, I'm not some punk kid that's calling you because I need a water bill paid, OK. I'm the guy that allocates these awards, and if I hang up the phone with you, it means that Tuesday afternoon the second alternate choice is going to get your $50,000. So if you want it, be courteous and kind with me, as I'm certainly set out to do with you. So let's start all over again, OK?*

Darlene Parker *Alright. What do I have to do?*

Robert Banks *OK, you simply have to be as courteous with me as I am certainly being with you and we won't have any problems, OK?*

The scammer, Robert Banks, is essentially saying, "I have the power" and is controlling the conversation. He wants his prospect to be submissive. The reason this works is that you have a conscience and the scammer doesn't.

In a *60 Minutes* interview that aired in 2004, a Canadian lottery scammer, discussed his methods and why he scammed the elderly. Here is what he had to say about his methods:

"I developed rapports with my customers. I called them my clients, who were really the victims. I spoke to them every day."

"I had to make the person on the other end of the phone feel like they were sitting in my office, but in a much

smaller chair on the other side of the desk. And I was the one who controlled their destiny. I was the one who could change their lives for them. I could make them happy. "

Here he explains why he did it:

"I was one of the best there was at conning people out of their life savings over a telephone. There is a perverse thrill to being able to do that to somebody. To be able to take somebody's hard-earned money. How does an athlete feel when they win a big event? How does a lawyer feel when they win a case in court? It was the same for us. When that check was sent and we received it, we won. "

Fraudsters also try to create a conducive environment for fraud before presenting their tactics. They do this because it makes their methods much more powerful and effective against the recipient – you. He's essentially priming you for his spiel. Cialdini, in his book *Pre-Suasion*, wrote that "…the psychological frame in which an appeal is first placed can carry equal or even greater weight." For those, like fraudsters, who want to be more influential, the "best persuaders become the best through 'pre-suasion.'" According to Cialdini, pre-suasion is "the process of arranging for recipients to be receptive to a message before they encounter it." He continues, "The basic idea of pre-suasion is that by guiding preliminary attention strategically, it's possible for a communicator to move recipients into agreement with a message before they experience it." It could be the use of a clever metaphor; a subtle push, rather than a more prominent one; creating an association; referencing a weakness early on to appear more honest; shared personal relationships (with God, for instance); coming from the same geographic location; ethnic commonality; and giving, seemingly, advice rather than opinion. These are strong, pre-suasive contexts for the scammer to utilize in order to get the recipient to assent to their pitch. In regard to metaphors, they are vivid and memorable, and impact our judgment, more than facts do. When people are drowning in information, metaphors help us cut to the chase. Fraudsters recognize that.

Schemes & Scams was written by special assistant attorney general Doug Shadel and former scammer "John T." In this 1994 book, "John T," stated, "…my favorite people to rip off were doctors and lawyers and highly educated people." He continued, "I think anyone in this country can be had by people like me on any given day." Finally, he stated, "The best targets are actually older women living alone."

Fraudsters follow current affairs closely, and will use these events in their pitch. For example, a popular scheme in the 1960s was mining for gold in the sea. SEALAB, an experimental underwater habitat developed by the U.S. Navy, was popular then, and helped cement the scam. The news tends to legitimize the pitch. The fraudsters cloak themselves in legitimacy. The cloak that is draped over the fraudster can be removed by asking probing questions, and gauging their reaction. They also are adept at adapting well geographically, plying their trade in Canada, then Jamaica, then Mumbai. As consumer protection laws improve in one jurisdiction, they move to another. What doesn't change, however, is that you – their victim – are only a phone call away. Fraudsters can set themselves up easily in the interconnected world of the internet. Investment scams can be done from anywhere in the world, the fraudster doesn't have to be in your neighborhood, although, with sophisticated technology, they can make it seem like they are. They can be hundreds or thousands of miles away. Fraudsters like low touch regulation, and are enamored of no regulation, and are now salivating at the prospect of reduced regulations and the concomitant weakening of regulatory powers.

The typical fraudster views you, like Harry Lime in *The Third Man* views his victim, as a dot. Lime is a black market racketeer operating in post World War II Vienna. One of his rackets is selling diluted medicine, resulting in patient deaths. The morally upright counterpoint to Lime is Holly Martins, a childhood friend, to whom he's offered a job. It's only later that Martins becomes aware of Lime's crimes. After being asked by Martins, played by Joseph Cotton, "Have you ever seen any of your victims?" Lime, played by Orson Welles, responds from the top of a Ferris Wheel surveying the passing crowd below, "Look down there. Tell me. Would you really feel any pity if one of those dots stopped moving forever? If I offered you twenty thousand pounds for every dot that stopped, would you really, old man, tell me to keep my money, or would you calculate how many dots you could afford to spare? Free of income tax old man." Martins remains steadfastly loyal to Lime and it's only after he learns more facts, and sees the results of his friend's actions, that he begins to widen his criticism of him. When he sees the dying victims in the hospital he becomes fully convinced of Lime's treachery. Sometimes, that's what it takes – an up close and personal view of the suffering. The dots have now become, at least in Martins eyes, human beings.

CHAPTER 16
Know Thyself

To them – the fraudsters – the victim has gone by many names: Boob, Chump, Dupe, Dummy, (the) Fleeced, Fool, Greenhorn, Loser, Mark, Mooch, Piker, Prey, Pushover, Sap, and Sucker.

In his book *Frauds, Swindles, and Rackets*, Robert Rosefsky discussed an advertisement that was placed in a periodical that simply stated: "Your Last Chance to Send $1," followed by an address. People sent in their dollar bills. Perhaps many of them didn't miss it, but the scammer was sure smiling. Through their "salami technique" the fraudsters took a little slice from a lot of curious men and women. But even before this scheme, many gullible investors in the late 19th and up to the mid 20th century bought the Brooklyn Bridge. One fraudulent seller – George C. Parker – sold it numerous times, and even persuaded purchasers that they could become rich by collecting tolls on it. And these victims went as far as erecting toll barriers, before the police interceded. These sales culminated in not only Parker's arrest, conviction, and imprisonment, but the turn of phrase, "if you believe that one, I have a bridge to sell you." Former Los Angeles County Sheriff Eugene Biscailuz, who is known for organizing the California Highway Patrol, gave a public service announcement before the airing of the 1952 film *Confidence Girl*. He asked the audience, "Would you believe it? People are still buying the Brooklyn Bridge. Yes, even as recently as this year. It's hard to believe, but true." Biscailuz, who still holds the record for the longest consecutive service in the Los Angeles County Sheriff's Department, noted that the victims were "successful citizens" who took the people trying to bilk them at face value and trusted them. In all schemes, the con man or woman is trying to sell you themselves. For if they are successful doing that, then they've got you hooked, and it'll be difficult to escape. Don't rely on trust. Rely on verified facts and verified documentation.

"Know thyself" is one of the Delphic maxims and was inscribed in the forecourt of the Temple of Apollo in Greece. What it means is that you need to be introspective and honest with yourself, and ask yourself open-ended questions, such as "Why am I making this investment?" "How well do I know this person?" and "Why do I trust this person?"

Don't ever think you won't be taken. We can all be taken. You decrease your odds of being fleeced by being aware of the problem and the developing scams, knowledgeable about the fraudster's approaches, and active in helping law enforcement solve this problem. If Victor Lustig can fool people using the same scam (he twice sold the Eiffel Tower) then it's certainly not inconceivable that you can be fooled, in matters of money, by a run-of-the-mill fraudster. Even the 18th President of the United States – Ulysses S. Grant – was swindled. In 1880 Grant's son Ulysses Jr., known as "Buck," and Ferdinand Ward, had opened a Wall Street brokerage house eponymously named Grant & Ward. In order to motivate investors, Ward paid them inordinately high interest, pledging the firm's securities. However, the interest Ward paid came from new investors, not from any firm profits. In 1881, Grant, impressed with the perceived success of the firm, invested $200,000, and became a limited partner. Grant & Ward lost money on speculative trades of its own and, in financial trouble, asked Grant for an additional investment. He borrowed to pony up more money. However, the securities the firm pledged as collateral were pledged on multiple loans. So, when these loans came due, there weren't enough securities, or cash, for that matter, to make the investors whole.

While the fraudster is the ultimate master in making the most of our human weaknesses, the investor is like the fish that only sees the worm, and not the hook that the worm is attached to. Be skeptical and find the flaws and risks, not just the upside promises. There's no need to rush. When you rush, you become impulsive. When you're impulsive you're not thinking deliberately and critically, and you'll make mistakes.

With certain frauds – like the online romance or sweetheart scam – we allow ourselves to believe what we want to believe, not what we should believe. We'd rather live in the fantasy, because it makes us happy, rather than the reality. Those who are victimized by this scam would rather be poorer and feel loved, than be richer yet feel unloved. We desire to be like Thurber's fictional character Walter Mitty. We don't need people to fool us, we fool ourselves. As the fraudster sucks us deeper and deeper into fantasy land, the harder it is for us to get back to reality. Remember what Leonardo da Vinci said. "It is easier to resist at the beginning than at the end." If that's the case, err on the side of caution, resist an offer up front, if you feel uneasy. Your gut's feeling may be your best instinct.

Most people focus on hits, rather than misses. It's easier to mentally account for the presence of something, rather than its absence. Take Mary Warren, whose story we discussed earlier. She didn't consider the losers that James might have had in picking stocks, focusing on the one winner he purportedly had in Apple Computer. If you're dealing with a victim ask them questions, always in a non-defensive and calm manner with the objective of planting doubts in their own mind and getting them to make the discovery that they've been scammed on their own. Those who have become victims hate the fact that they are sitting on losses, so they are desperate to recoup their losses to become whole, so they keep throwing good money after bad. (Daniel Kahneman, who trained as a psychologist, won the

Nobel Prize in Economic Sciences in 2002 for "prospect theory," which concerns the greater weight people assign to losses as compared with gains.) Because people have a strong desire to make up losses if they are being conned, they are vulnerable to another scam.

We are busy and sometimes lazy. There's only so much we can do in a day. But it's critical we don't take shortcuts when it comes to investing our money. We don't look forward to spending countless hours trying to make a decision, so we expedite things, and the fraudster counts on this. In addition, con artists are strong personalities (remember Robert Banks from the previous chapter) who exploit the "follower mentality." As a senior's physical and mental health diminishes, they tend to lose self-confidence and easily fall into this role. Help the senior by increasing their self-confidence in their own abilities. Don't be embarrassed to come forward and report your experiences if you've been victimized. It's not your fault. Coming forward demonstrates your courage and resolve to bring the scammers to justice. Also, don't worry about being polite. You're not dealing with a lady or gentleman in the fraudster. We also have a tendency to abbreviate our decision making process. We are satisfied with what we believe is good enough. Another Nobel laureate in Economics, Herbert Simon, referred to this as "satisficing" – a portmanteau of the words satisfy and suffice.

Victims fall for the herd mentality. Think for yourself. Don't play "Follow the leader," which is for children. The psychological makeup of an impulsive and uncritical investor is one that doesn't want to miss out on something. They want to feel special, like they're part of something, like Bernie Madoff's investors before they became victims. Be introspective. If you don't understand an investment, then take a pass. If they push the urgency of getting the deal done, like a used car salesman, then pass. Talk an investment over with someone you trust, but never with someone who has made the investment, as their opinion is innately biased and a clear conflict of interest.

Don't take a cavalier and nonchalant attitude when picking a financial adviser. Do your homework. If you aren't good at picking investments, you must at least be good at selecting an advisor. Do a Google search. Don't be hesitant to ask for a resume. If they have certifications, like the Certified Financial Planner (CFP), then verify that they are in good standing and active. Look at FINRA's BrokerCheck, which you can do here: https://brokercheck.finra.org. Call the state securities regulator. Rely less on any references.

Never give an advisor or broker control of your money. The money should be at a qualified and independent bank, broker-dealer, or custodian. Never make a check out to your broker or advisor. This should only be made out to the reputable bank, broker-dealer, or custodian. Don't give your advisor or broker check writing powers. Ask your advisor or broker about their greatest investment mistake and how it happened. If they don't have one, be suspicious. Even the world's greatest investor – Warren Buffett – will tell you he has many. Know the websites of your financial institutions and, when you need to access them, go there directly. Beware that many criminals have set-up similarly sounding websites, essentially masquerading as legitimate financial institutions, but have changed important details like telephone numbers and email addresses on these fake sites. This will be used to get your personal information and money.

We are all greedy to some extent, and fraudsters know that of victims, although most of us, unlike fraudsters, have a limit to how far we'd go for what we want. Don't try to keep up with the Joneses or compare yourself to others. If you do, you'll always feel like you'll never have enough wealth, so you reach for that extra yield by taking risks with unscrupulous people.

Rational choice theory, which derives from classical economics, posits that individuals make prudent and logical decisions, i.e., they act rationally. The more recent and influential behavioral economists disagree. They say that we are, contrary to the classical theory of economics, irrational. We are affected by our biases, and, therefore, make mental short cuts (again, known as "heuristics" in the scientific field) to make decision or judgments. For instance, one bias we've discussed and may have is "representativeness." Take the recent "Can you tell the difference?" commercial from LetsMakeAPlan.org. On January 9, 2014, in Dallas, Texas, a well-dressed and groomed man appears in a conference room with individual, prospective financial clients and says, "Let me talk to you about retirement. The 401(k) is the most sound way to go. But let's talk about asset allocation," then asks "Would you trust me as your financial advisor?" After getting assent from each of them, he exposes his secret. "I'm actually a DJ." After shimming around the conference room he says, "I have no financial experience at all." The DJ was representative of a financial advisor. He was in the typical environment – a professional looking conference room. He was dressed and groomed liked the typical financial advisor, with a suit and tie, shiny shoes, and a neat haircut and no facial hair. Yet, he wasn't a financial advisor. Representativeness does not equal fact. We make easy associations. If a fraudster has an expensive car, then he must be a great investor. This is known as "value attribution" the tendency to imbue someone with certain qualities based on perceived value rather that objective data. Are we going to make a critical decision based on this one piece of information? Most of the time we don't use all available relevant data, but only what we believe is a representative piece of the total.

Before falling victim to the fraudster, we fall victim to our own biases. For example, with "confirmation bias," we make up our mind and then just look at the factors that support that decision, rather than contradictory information. It's akin to listening to what conversations, or pieces of conversations, we want to during a party, whether they are in our circle of acquaintances or not (the so-called "cocktail party effect"). Let your defining emotion be doubt.

With "framing bias," sometimes people tend to care more about a story than numbers, or other relevant facts. Framing bias is a tendency for us to behave differently depending on how a situation is presented to us. Sometimes human judgment is distorted by the memorable. Mary Warren was taken by James D. Smith's first name. Why? Because her deceased husband's first name was James.

In order to de-bias our judgments, according to Cialdini, ask, "What future events could make this plan go wrong?" and "What would happen to me if it did go wrong?" Again, critical, deliberate analysis may keep us out of the fraudster's traps.

PART IV
Fighting Back

CHAPTER 17
A Fraud Fighter's Tools of the Trade

Fraud fighters are frustrated. It seems like fighting fraudsters is an uphill battle, and the hill is steep. Consider the words of Doug Shadel in his book *Scams & Schemes*, about his empathy toward an investment fraud victim, "I just cannot describe the anguish I felt for her and the deep sense of helplessness over not being able to get her back her money." Law enforcement focuses on education and prevention. "Why?" you ask. Since many frauds originate from overseas, there is either no subpoena authority, or limited authority, and insufficient human resources. It's an environment where law enforcement can't easily investigate and prosecute. But that doesn't mean we stop trying. We don't.

Part of how we fight back is conducting a due diligence investigation that culminates in a report for use by law enforcement authorities. An investigation involves obtaining evidence, creating a report, and testifying. Part of evidence gathering includes speaking to witnesses, and other knowledgeable third parties who are well-versed in a particular industry, as well as using online tools. While the methods of conducting an investigation and report writing are beyond the scope of this book, I would like to introduce you to some basic online tools that are free. Of course there are other commercial database vendors that charge a fee. You may find the tools below helpful as part of doing basic, and preliminary, due diligence on an individual or company.

Google Search

This may be the most basic way to find information on the internet. Although Google is the most used search engine, it isn't the only one. There are others, like Microsoft's Bing,

DuckDuckGo, and Dogpile, which is a metasearch engine that aggregates results from other search engines before providing its results to you.

When searching for an individual or firm using Google, you can narrow your search to "News," "Videos," or "Images," for example. You can also narrow the time range of your search by using "Tools" and then using the "Any time" drop down menu.

If you want to search for an exact phrase, then put that phrase in quotation marks. (For example: "investment scam"). You can also exclude terms from your search results by putting a minus sign immediately before the word you'd like to exclude. (For example: "investment scam" –Madoff). To get details about a specific website, then put "info:" in front of the site address. (For example: info: www.ponzitracker.com). Put an asterisk in your word or phrase where you want to leave a placeholder, in order to search for wildcards or unknown words. (For example, "largest * fraud" would return web pages containing "largest" followed by one or more words followed by "fraud.") You can use "link:" and the minus sign operator in order to obtain pages that link to a particular website, excluding links that website makes to itself. (For example: link: www.ponzitracker.com – www.ponzitracker.com). If you are searching for a particular file type, such as .doc, .pdf, or .jpg, for instance, then you can use the "filetype:" operator. (For example: filetype:doc "consumer fraud" will return only .doc results containing the exact phrase "consumer fraud").

Access the tool here: https://www.google.com

LinkedIn

There are many social network websites, such as Facebook, Twitter, and Instagram. LinkedIn, which has been around since

2003 and is now owned by Microsoft, is a business-oriented professional social network. According to its Form 10-Q, as of September 30, 2016, LinkedIn, which is available in many languages, had nearly 467 million accounts globally. It allows members (both workers and employers) to create profiles, after which they can connect with each other. All content on LinkedIn is tagged, which means that the content is indexed and searchable. For individuals, LinkedIn is essentially an online resume. You can view someone's experience, education, certifications, honors and awards, interests, accomplishments, and featured skills and endorsements. If you are one of a LinkedIn user's connections, then you can also view any posts they've made to the site. You may also be able to see their connections, if not designated as private. If it is designated as private, then you can see some of their connections – those that have endorsed them for skills. Note that the information in someone's profile is derived from the individual or one or more of their connections; none of this information is verified. LinkedIn allows you to view employers and the people that work there, as well as their posts, without having to be connected with them.

Access the tool here: https://www.linkedin.com

Certified Financial Planner Search Tool

There are many designations that a broker or financial advisor may use. Some are well-regarded, because they require studying rigorously, passing an exam, taking continuing education credits to maintain it, and adhering to ethical standards. Others are not. The CFP, CFA, and CPA are in the former camp. The Certified Financial Planner Board of Standards, which was founded in 1985 as a 501(c)(3) non-profit organization, sponsors the Certified Financial Planner (CFP) certification, and enforces the requirements needed to obtain and maintain it, including those pertaining to education, examination, experience, and ethics. With this tool, you can verify someone's CFP certification status, and whether they have any CFP Board disciplinary history or bankruptcy disclosure within the last 10 years.

Access the tool here:

http://www.cfp.net/utility/verify-an-individual-s-cfp-certification-and-background

CFA Institute CFA Charterholder Search

The CFA Institute is a global association of investment professionals. It offers the Chartered Financial Analyst (CFA) designation, which was created in 1962, at the same time it created a code of conduct. Since then, 120,000 CFA Charters have been awarded.

Access the tool here:

https://www.cfainstitute.org/community/membership/directory/pages/results.aspx

CPAVerify

CPAVerify is an online central repository of information about licensed Certified Public Accountants (CPAs) and public accounting firms maintained by the National Association of State Boards of Accountancy (NASBA) to provide a single-search resource covering participating jurisdictions where a person or firm has been licensed.

Access the tool here: https://cpaverify.org/

FINRA BrokerCheck Search Tool

This tool, which is from the Financial Industry Regulatory Authority (FINRA) – a self-regulatory organization for the U.S.

securities industry – can help you search the background of your broker and brokerage firm, as well as advisor and investment adviser firm.

For brokers, you'll be able to see: (1) if they're registered, which requires that they pass an exam, and be employed with a brokerage firm; (2) if they have any disclosure events, such as customer complaints, legal settlements with clients, arbitrations, employment terminations for cause, personal bankruptcy filing, regulatory actions, or any civil or criminal proceedings; (3) the industry-related exams they've passed; their current and/or past employers; and (4) other business activities they may be involved in. Check out that there not only actively licensed, but licensed in good standing.

For brokerage firms, you'll be able to see: (1) the firm's basic profile – what kind of entity it is, where it was formed, and when; (2) what regulators, and exchanges, they're registered with; (3) the types of business activities they conduct; and (3) any disclosure events, such as civil or criminal proceedings, or regulatory actions. However, you won't see any legal settlements with clients.

Access the tool here: https://brokercheck.finra.org

SEC Investment Adviser Public Disclosure Tool

This tool, which is derived from the Securities and Exchange Commission's Investment Adviser Registration Depository, also feeds FINRA's BrokerCheck.

For advisors, you'll be able to see: (1) current employer, including state where they are registered to do business; (2) past employers, and registration history with other investment adviser firms; (3) industry exams they've passed; and (4) professional designations they've reported, and disclosure information.

For investment adviser firms that are registered with the SEC, you'll be able to see their Form-ADV ("Uniform Application For Investment Adviser Registration and Report By Exempt Reporting Advisers") and Form-ADV Part 2A Brochure. Not all advisers are required to register with the SEC. The Form-ADV contains (1) the entity's full legal name, address, and contact phone number; (2) the number of employees they have; (3) the types of clients they advise; (4) the different ways they are compensated for their advice; (5) the dollar value of their assets under management (AUM), and the number of clients they have; (6) the types of advisory activities they conduct; (7) the types of other business activities they conduct; (8) disciplinary history; and (9) the names of owners and executive officers.

Under SEC rules, an investment adviser firm is required to deliver to current and prospective clients a brochure disclosing information about their firm. This "Part 2A Brochure," which is designed to be consumer friendly, contains a narrative description of: (1) any material business changes since the issuance of the last brochure; (2) the types of advisory services offered; (3) fees and compensation; (4) whether client accounts are periodically reviewed; (4) information about the custody of clients assets; (5) under certain circumstances, balance sheet information; and (6) other information noted on the Form-ADV, but in more detail.

As for custody, if you're selecting an investment adviser firm to manage your money, then you don't want them to maintain custody of your assets. Your funds should be held with an independent and qualified bank, broker-dealer, or custodian that sends you account statements directly, and at least quarterly. Review these statements carefully.

Access the tool here:
https://www.adviserinfo.sec.gov/IAPD/IAPDSearch.aspx

NFA BASIC

The National Futures Association (NFA), which is a self-regulatory organization for the futures industry, maintains the Background Affiliation Status Information Center (BASIC). If you are an investor who is contemplating opening an account to trade futures, then you can check out the individual (e.g., "Introducing Broker") and firm (e.g., Commodity Trading Advisor) you are contemplating trading through or with. Futures are exchange-traded financial contracts that obligate the buyer and seller to transact in a certain quantity of a physical commodity, such as corn, gold, crude oil, or wheat, or a financial instrument, such as currencies, stock indices, or US Treasuries, at a predetermined future date and price.

Access the tool here:
http://www.nfa.futures.org/BasicNet/Welcome.aspx

SEC EDGAR Search Tools

The SEC's Electronic Data Gathering Analysis and Retrieval (EDGAR) system, which began collecting documents in 1984, is a database of forms for those companies and others who are required by law to file them with the SEC. EDGAR contains 21 million filings. Since 1934, when it was created, the SEC has required disclosure in forms and documents. Because securities law is premised on disclosure, the purpose of this database is to enhance the efficiency and fairness of the securities market for the benefit of investors, corporations, and the economy by accelerating the dissemination of this information for analysis. EDGAR electronically holds: (1) public company financial information, such as Form 10-K, which contains audited annual financial statements; (2) executive compensation information, as included in Schedule 14A (annual proxy statement) and other forms; (3) insider transactions and beneficial ownership interest information for corporate insiders, i.e., officers, directors, and 10% owners, as contained in Form 3, which is an initial statement of beneficial ownership, and other forms; (4) shareholder meetings and proxy solicitations information; (5) business combination information, including mergers and acquisitions when one or both of the companies involved are subject to the SEC disclosure rules; (6) initial public offering or IPO information in the form of the registration statement filed by the new issuer; (7) bankruptcy information as disclosed in Form 8-K, which is a report of current material information; (8) mutual fund product information; (9) variable insurance product information; and (10) Form D, which is a notice of an exempt offering of securities. While the SEC does not require companies that are raising less than $1 million under Rule 504 of Regulation D to be "registered" with the SEC, these companies are required to file a Form D. It serves as a brief notice that provides information about the company and the offering.

Access the tools here: https://www.sec.gov/edgar/searchedgar/webusers.htm.

CSA SEDAR Tool

Like the SEC, the Canadian Securities Administrators (CSA) developed its own database to provide access to most public securities documents, including those for companies and investment funds, and information filed by issuers with the thirteen provincial and territorial securities regulatory authorities in Canada. The database is the System for Electronic Document Analysis and Retrieval (SEDAR).

Access the tool here: https://www.sedar.com/search/search_en.htm

SearchSystems.net

The World Wide Web or simply the "Web", which was invented by Tim-Berners Lee, is a method of accessing the internet. For instance, in many places of this book, I provide, through an https:// address, many resources located on the internet. There are many public record databases that may be useful when conducting a due diligence review of an individual or firm. These databases can best be accessed by going through SearchSystems.net, which is the best resource for public records, particularly criminal records, on the internet.

In 1996 there were only a very small number of public record databases on the internet, and they were difficult to find. Today, SearchSystems,net has organized them in a way that facilitates a user's search. Since they started this service, they have found and added over 55,000 links to public record databases. These links are organized by geographic location and by type of public record, and a description has been added to each one. SearchSystems.net adds new databases each day.

The site is fairly easy to use. Start at their "Home" page. It's organized primarily by geographic location, so if you're looking for records in Florida, for example, use the "Search Free Public Records" tools at the top of the page. Use the drop-down menu called "By State" to select Florida. Or, simply scroll down to "Search By State" and select Florida. This will bring you to "Florida Public Records." The links there are statewide resources. If you're looking for information in a particular city or county in Florida, then use the links at the top left of the Florida Public Records page, or use the search fields for "By County" or "By City" at the Home page of the site in the "Search Free Public Records" tool bar.

You can locate the county directories even if you don't know the corresponding county for a city. To do this, use the search field called "By City" in the tool bar at the top of the page. Type in "Naples" and click on the match for "Naples, FL" that will appear below. The next page will have links to any Naples databases, and the corresponding county databases (Collier County). There is some basic county information concerning population, demographics, home values, and per capita income, as well as a list of libraries that may be used for further research.

You can also start with "Search By Category" from the Home page. So you can select "Licenses" or "Corporations & Companies," for example, among many categories, and then select the state you're interested in.

Access the tool here:
http://publicrecords.searchsystems.net/

FINRA Arbitration Awards Online

FINRA maintains a database of arbitration awards from May 1989 to the present. These include historical arbitration awards from the NASD (FINRA's predecessor organization), the New York Stock Exchange, the American Stock Exchange, the Philadelphia Stock Exchange, and the Municipal Securities Rulemaking Board. FINRA encourages parties to perform independent research to determine whether a court has vacated, confirmed, or modified a prospective arbitrator's past awards. FINRA further cautions that the database may not reflect whether a party has appealed an order or the outcome of any such appeal.

Access the tool here: https://www.finra.org/arbitration-and-mediation/arbitration-awards

FINRA Disciplinary Actions Online

FINRA maintains a database of any disciplinary actions

brought against any of its member brokerage firms or brokers that were issued during 2005 or later and are eligible for publication. Prior to December 16, 2013 disclosure of disciplinary actions were limited to those resulting in sanctions of $10,000 or more. More actions, at FINRA's discretion, are reported now.

Access the tool here: https://disciplinaryactions.finra.org/

Whois Lookup

This is a website domain search tool. It will provide information about a web domain, a subcategory of which are web address or Uniform Resource Locator (URL). For example, https://www.google.com. This tool provides relevant email addresses and, if the company you're dealing with is fraudulent, it may contain the names of the fraudsters behind it. It also lets you see the date the website domain was created.

Access the tool here: https://whois.domaintools.com/

Internet Archive Wayback Machine

The Wayback Machine, which was launched by the nonprofit Internet Archive in 2001, is a digital archive of the World Wide Web and other information on the internet. The vision of the Wayback Machine is to capture and archive all content on the internet that otherwise would be lost whenever a site is modified or shuts down. If a website domain is no longer active, you may be able to still view some of their archived webpages with this tool. Also, you can capture a webpage as it appears at the time you access it for use as a trusted citation in the future by using this tool.

Access the tool here: https://archive.org/web/

IRS EO Select Check

The Internal Revenue Service has an Exempt Organizations (EO) Select Check online search tool that allows users to search for and select an exempt organization and check certain information about its federal tax status and filings.

Access the tool here: https://apps.irs.gov/app/eos/

Federal Bureau of Prisons Inmate Search

The Federal Bureau of Prisons, which is part of the U.S. Department of Justice, is responsible for the custody and care of over 188,000 federal prisoners. You can search for current or past inmates.

Access the tool here: https://www.bop.gov/inmateloc/

AARP Scam-Tracking Map

The American Association of Retired Persons (AARP) maintains on its website (1) a list of law enforcement alerts for each state, and Puerto Rico, the US Virgin Island, and Guam and (2) an interactive map that when clicked on will show scams reported by individuals to the AARP.

Access the tool here: https://action.aarp.org/site/SPageNavigator/FraudMap.html

White Collar Crime Early Warning System (WCCEWS)

The term "white collar" crime was coined by Edwin H. Sutherland, a noted sociologist, in a 1940 speech he gave entitled, "White Collar Criminality," which was printed in the *American Sociological Review*. "White-collar" crime is a nonviolent crime motivated by financial gain, such as fraud, that is committed by a seemingly professional business person.

WCCEWS is based on data going back to 1964 that was provided by the Financial Industry Regulatory Authority (FINRA), which is the self-regulator for the securities industry in the US. The system is designed to identify geographic zones that are at high risk for "white collar" crime. Those zones are in red. According to its developers, it can be used for citizen policing and awareness. However, the system doesn't identify those individuals within a certain region that are likely to commit a financial crime. Not yet. The developers are planning to enhance the system with facial analysis and psychometrics, which is a field of study concerned with measuring certain aspects of a person's psychological make-up, such as attitude, knowledge, and personality. The developers are attempting to derive a psychological assessment of a typical "white collar" criminal, and compare it to one who doesn't commit such crimes.

Access the tool here:
https://whitecollar.thenewinquiry.com/

The resources I have provided above are non-exhaustive. The Association of Certified Fraud Examiners (ACFE) has published a list of "Useful Websites," and, even, this is not a complete list of the resources you can use when conducting due diligence. These "Useful Websites" can be accessed here:

http://www.acfe.com/uploadedFiles/ACFE_Website/Co ntent/documents/sample-documents/Useful-Websites-2014.pdf

CHAPTER 18
Recommendations

Make Finance/Economics a required high school course. The problem of elder financial abuse can best be handled proactively. And that starts before we are aged, and at our most vulnerable. Let's make Finance/Economics a required course in high schools. According to the Survey of the States, currently, only 17 states require it. The curriculum must include the discussion of financial frauds. As a practical matter, finance concerns all of us, as does being subjected to fraud, no matter what profession we ultimately choose. We need the knowledge that finance brings, so that we are better equipped with the tools to better fight fraud when it comes knocking at our door.

Get seniors out and about, socializing, instead of being stuck at home. Local shuttle service to senior centers and other venues will help seniors engage with others in the community. For example, the Town of North Hempstead in Nassau County, New York has "Project Independence," which connects seniors to exercise classes and various social groups and provides discounted and free transportation to medical appointments and grocery shopping, respectively. Being locked up at home only makes them more accessible when the scammer calls. Visit your elder family members regularly, and inquire into their well-being, and monitor for any unusually signs that may indicate elder financial abuse.

Authorities should take quick action, including notification and training, when they learn about a scam. Local communities should be reaching out, via telephone and email, to warn their residents about the latest scam. Notifications occur with severe weather storms; they should occur with fraudulent financial storms as well. Since the criminal is constantly refining the frauds they commit, law enforcement, lawmakers, and other fraud fighters must warn seniors, and the senior's family and friends, as quickly as possible. The means of outreach should be varied, and include scam prevention events at libraries and other local venues. Training should be a two-way street. You want to hear from the senior as much as they hear from you. You want to find out their concerns, and what's worrying them. In regard to training, some fraud fighter's use a pretend scam to prevent a real one. Some might act out a scenario. It's important to get the audience's feedback. Training, as well as other preventative measures, offer better returns, than fighting fraudsters after they've made off with the money.

Pass the Senior Safe Act. This legislation was re-introduced recently by Senator Susan Collins (Republican-Maine). This legislation would encourage financial institutions to report incidents of elder financial abuse by shielding them from lawsuits when they make good faith reporting to the authorities. While regulators disagree, financial institutions believe that they would be violating the privacy provisions if they were to report elder financial abuse to a third-party, such as Adult Protective Services. In order to get the "safe harbor," financial institutions would have to train their employees on flagging abuse when they see it. Until this legislation is passed, financial services personnel, especially client-facing employees, should look out for the hallmarks of elder financial abuse and report it.

In addition to the Senior Safe Act, states and the federal government, need stronger laws to protect seniors, who are vulnerable. According to *Fraud*, since the late 19th century judges have argued that aged individuals deserve greater legal safeguards because of their declining mental faculties, among other reasons. It's time for legislatures to recognize this vulnerability by implementing tougher penalties against those defrauding seniors.

All financial institutions, including money services businesses, should train their front-line employees to spot elder financial abuse, and the institutions should report it when suspected. Financial institutions, because of the close role they have with their customers, are uniquely positioned to spot elder financial exploitation, and report it. They may become aware of elder financial abuse either directly, by contact with their customer, or indirectly, by noticing banking patterns being perpetrated by a potential fraudster. On February 22, 2011, the Financial Crimes Enforcement Network (FinCEN), which is a financial intelligence unit within the U.S. Treasury Department, released "Advisory to Financial Institutions on Filing Suspicious Activity Reports Regarding Elder Financial Exploitation." FinCEN believes that erratic or unusual banking transactions, or changes in banking patterns may give rise to the senior being exploited financially. This may include frequent large withdrawals, including daily maximum currency withdrawals from an ATM; sudden Non-Sufficient Fund (NSF) activity; uncharacteristic nonpayment for services, which may indicate a loss of funds or access to funds; debit transactions that are inconsistent for the elder; uncharacteristic attempts to wire large sums of money; and closing of CDs or accounts without regard to penalties, as occurred with the fictional Mary Warren earlier in the book. In addition, FinCEN believes that certain interactions with the customer, and caregiver, might indicate red-flags that need to be followed-up on by the financial institution. Such red flags include: situations where a caregiver or other individual shows excessive interest in the elder's finances or assets, does not allow the elder to speak for himself, or is reluctant to leave the elder's side during conversations; the elder shows an unusual degree of fear or submissiveness toward a caregiver, or expresses a fear of eviction or nursing home placement if money is not given to a caretaker; the financial institution is unable to speak directly with the elder, despite repeated attempts to contact him or her; a new caretaker, relative, or friend suddenly begins conducting financial transactions on behalf of the elder without proper documentation; the customer moves away from existing relationships and toward new associations with other "friends" or strangers; the elderly individual's financial management changes suddenly, such as through a change of power of attorney to a different family member or a new individual; the elderly customer lacks knowledge about his or her financial status, or shows a sudden reluctance to discuss financial matters.

The financial institution should follow-up on red-flags by discerning all available, and relevant, facts and circumstances. After having done this, if they have so much as reason to suspect that a transaction has no business or apparent lawful purpose or is not the sort in which the particular customer would normally be expected to engage, and the financial institution knows of no reasonable explanation for the transaction, then they should file a Suspicious Activity Report. A SAR is a document that financial institutions are required to file with the government when they suspect elder financial abuse has been committed against one of their customers, among other circumstances. It's important, in order to facilitate follow-up by criminal enforcement authorities, that financial institutions select the appropriate characterization of suspicious activity (e.g., "Embezzlement/theft," "Forgery," "Significant wire or other transactions without economic purpose") in the "Suspicious Activity Information" section of the SAR form. In addition, they should include the term "elder financial exploitation" in the narrative portion of the form. The narrative should also include an explanation of why they are making the report. FinCEN notes that the potential victim of elder financial exploitation should not be reported as the subject of the SAR. Instead, all available, and relevant, information on the victim should be included in the narrative portion of the SAR. After the release of the advisory, FinCEN noted that most

SAR activity resulted from "patterns of financial exploitation perpetrated by a relative or caregiver against elderly victims." Accompanying narratives with the SAR "described the perpetrator coercing or cajoling the victim into completing financial transactions that benefited the perpetrator at the expense of the victim." And, in other circumstances, "the perpetrator reportedly abused his/her power of attorney over the victim's account." There was also "unusual wire activity by their elderly customers, including multiple same-day wire transfers, sometimes from different agent locations, to different cities in the United States, as well as unusual wires to moderate and/or high-risk countries," with these filings describing the senior being subjected to a scam, including the online romance or sweetheart scam.

In March 2016, the Consumer Financial Protection Bureau (CFPB), an agency of the US government that was formed in July 2011 to oversees financial institutions' adherence to consumer financial protection laws issued, "Recommendations and Report for Financial Institutions on Preventing and Responding to Elder Financial Exploitation," and accompanying "Advisory for Financial Institutions on Preventing and Responding to Elder Financial Exploitation." Among other things, the CFPB tells financial institutions that they should be aware of the 2013 guidance "from eight federal financial regulators that clarifies that reporting financial abuse of older adults to appropriate local, state and federal authorities does not, in general, violate the privacy provisions of [the Gramm-Leach-Bliley Act]" and stated that "[s]everal state regulators issued similar guidance," so they recommend that all cases of suspected elder financial exploitation be reported to the relevant federal, state and local authorities.

In addition to the red-flags noted by FinCEN, the CFPB noted these hallmarks of elder financial exploitation for account-related activity: large gaps in check numbers, or "out of sync" check numbers; abrupt changes to financial documents, such as a new power of attorney, a change to a joint account or a change in account beneficiary; excessive numbers of payments or payments of large sums to a caregiver or third party; new account use soon after adding an authorized user; statements mailed to an address separate from customer's residence; new activity on an inactive account or joint account; and signatures that do not match or appear suspicious. As well, with regard to interactions with older consumers, caregivers and other third parties, CFPB noted these additional red flags, beyond those provided by FinCEN: a previously uninvolved relative, caregiver or friend begins conducting financial transactions on behalf of an older consumer—or claims access or privileges to the consumer's private information—without proper documentation; an older consumer exhibits an unusual degree of fear, anxiety, submissiveness or deference to a caregiver or other third party; an older person expresses excitement over a financial opportunity, prize, or windfall; and an older consumer appears to neglect or experience a decline in appearance, grooming, or hygiene. It's important to remember that these hallmarks of financial elder abuse aren't exhaustive.

The CFPB recommends that financial institutions tweak their fraud detection systems in order to include analyses of the types of products and account activity that may be associated with the risk of elder financial exploitation, and states that they should use predictive analytics to review their filtering criteria against elder account holders' patterns so that they can identify additional risk factors that may be associated with elder financial exploitation.

The CFPB encourages financial institutions to offer elder-friendly accounts, including protective opt-in account features, such as cash withdrawal limits, geographic transaction limits, alerts for specified account activity, and read-only or view-only access to accounts for authorized third parties, such as a trusted family member who can monitor the senior's account for irregularities without having access to the senior's funds or the ability to engage in transactions.

In March 2017, FINRA received approval from the SEC on a rule proposal that is designed to address financial exploitation of seniors (those 65 and older). The rule, which goes into effect in February 2018, involves two measures to protect senior investors: it would require brokerage firms "to make reasonable efforts to obtain the name and contact information for a trusted contact person for a [senior] customer's account" and allows such firms "to place a temporary hold on a disbursement of funds or securities when there is reasonable belief of financial exploitation," according to FINRA. Generally, simply asking a senior for the name and contact information of a trusted contact person would be deemed "reasonable efforts," and would satisfy the rule's requirements. The trusted contact person must be age 18 or older. Brokerage firms are required to let seniors know, in writing, that they are authorized to contact the trusted person and disclose information about their account to address possible financial exploitation. FINRA believes that customers may benefit from this rule under a number of circumstances, such as when the firm is unable to reach the customer after numerous efforts, when the customer is having health issues and is hospitalized, or when a customer is suffering from Alzheimer's disease.

Brokerage firms should be aware that a senior customer's request to change his or her trusted contact person may be a possible red flag of financial exploitation. For example, a senior instructing their broker to change their trusted contact person from an immediate family member to a previously unknown third party may be a red flag of financial exploitation. In such circumstances, a filing of a suspicious activity report may be required.

While a temporary hold may be placed on a particular suspicious disbursement, a brokerage firm cannot place one on non-suspicious disbursements. In addition, holds cannot be placed on securities trades. So, if a senior sells their stock, the order will be executed. However, if they sold their stock, and asked that the proceeds of the sale be disbursed out of their account, while there is a reasonable belief of financial exploitation, then the disbursement may be held up. Notification of any held disbursements, and the reason for such, must be provided to the trusted contact person and the customer by the brokerage firm no later than two business days after placing the hold.

Calls into FINRA's "Securities Helpline for Seniors" prompted the need for the proposal. Since April 2015, when the hotline was launched, it has received more than 9,200 calls from all 50 states, and secured $4.3 million in voluntary reimbursements to callers. According to Robert W. Cook, FINRA President and CEO, "These rules will provide firms with tools to respond more quickly and effectively to protect seniors from financial exploitation."

Make final the Federal Communications Commission proposal that is designed to weaken the ability of scammers to utilize spoofed robocalls. Consumer groups, the telecommunications industry, and the federal government should continue taking steps to tackle the robocall problem.

Federal criminal enforcement authorities should step up cooperation with their foreign counterparts to shut down scam call center operations more quickly. Many recent scams can be traced to Indian call centers. In October

2016, police in a Mumbai suburb raided three office buildings suspected of being used to make the fraudulent IRS scam calls and detained hundreds for questioning. According to the *Los Angeles Times*, Sagar Thakkar, known as "Shaggy," the 24-year old ringleader of the operation, was among those indicted for conspiracy, fraud, and money laundering. Although there was growing concern in both the U.S. and India, according to the *Los Angeles Times*, the scam continued for several years. Its reported take was $100 million, according to *The New York Times*. Law enforcement cannot allow these scammers to operate with impunity for so long. Most of the law enforcement in the telemarketing and internet realm in the 1990s and 2000s involved targeting domestic fraudulent operators. For example, the FBI had success with its Operation Disconnect (1991), which resulted in 240 arrests, Operation Sunstroke (1993), culminating in Operation Senior Sentinel (1995), which resulted in 1,200 arrests, and Operation Double Barrel (1998), which sought to create greater coordination between the U.S. Department of Justice, Federal Trade Commission (FTC), and other federal agencies to bring both criminal and civil enforcement actions against telemarketing schemes. In addition, Project Jackpot (1996) was a major enforcement effort targeting firms that fraudulently offered purportedly valuable prizes to consumers to induce them to purchase products. It culminated in eight law enforcement actions from the FTC, five from the U.S. Postal Service, and forty-three from the U.S. states' Attorneys General. Operation Top 10 Dot- Cons (2000) was a 10-month-long operation involving law enforcement officials from the U.S. and eight other countries, targeting the top 10 dot-cons, including internet auction fraud, which was the top consumer complaint at the time. Legal actions were brought against 251 scammers. The FTC and twenty-nine U.S. states' Attorneys General, in Operation Bidder Beware (2003), launched a law enforcement crackdown targeting internet auction scams that bilked thousands of consumers out of their money and merchandise. It resulted in fifty-seven criminal and civil law enforcement actions. Another major law enforcement campaign was Operation Empty Promises (2011) an initiative that stepped up an ongoing campaign against scammers who falsely promised guaranteed jobs and opportunities to "be your own boss" to consumers who were struggling with unemployment and diminished incomes as a consequence of the economic downturn at the time. It resulted in more than ninety enforcement actions. Even after the action in Mumbai, these scams are still alive and well. Personally, I see a high level of fraudulent call activity.

Federal criminal enforcement authorities should better coordinate with state and local authorities, as well as industry professionals. One success has been the "Security Summit" a group of federal, state, and tax preparation industry officials who discuss and share information on the latest scams in the tax fraud area.

Target high-risk geographic areas that have a concentration of seniors for enforcement. As recommended by the National Elder Mistreatment Study, dedicated resources and civil remedies should be directed toward this type of mistreatment (e.g., prosecutors assigned to handling financial abuse cases in geographic regions with high numbers of older adults).

RESOURCES

Select Contacts:

For Emergencies Only: 9-1-1

To locate Adult Protective Services for a particular area:

1-800-677-1116

Annual Credit Report –

https://www.annualcreditreport.com; 1-877- 322-8228

Federal Bureau of Investigation – https://www.fbi.gov

Federal Trade Commission – https://www.ftc.gov; 1-877-382-4357 (for unfair business practices; to obtain educational material on scams)

1-877-ID-THEFT (1-877-438-4338)

(for ID theft)

spam@uce.gov (email for forwarding unwanted or deceptive spam to the FTC).

National Do Not Call Registry –

https://www.donotcall.gov; 1-888-382-1222

U.S. Postal Service – https://www.uspsoig.gov; 1-888-877-7644

National Committee for the Prevention of Elder Abuse –

https://www.preventelderabuse.org; 1-202-464-9481

Elder Financial Protection Network –

http://www.elderfinancialprotection.org/; 1-707-981-8403

National Center on Elder Abuse –

https://www.ncea.aoa.gov; 1-855-500-3537 (ELDR)

National Council on Aging – https://www.ncoa.org; 1-202-479-1200

National Consumers League'sFRAUD!ORG

https://www.fraud.org (to sign up for fraud alerts and/or submit a complaint)

The Partnership For Safe Medicines –

https://www.safemedicines.org; 1-703-679-7233 (SAFE)

Better Business Bureau – https://www.newyork.bbb.org

Securities and Exchange Commission (SEC) –

https://www.sec.gov; 1-800-732-0330 (for filing securities fraud complaints)

Financial Industry Regulatory Authority (FINRA) –

https://www.finra.org; 1-800-289-9999 (for checking out broker-dealers, advisory firms, stockbrokers, and advisors)

FINRA's Securities Helpline for Seniors – 1-844-574-3577

North American Securities Administrators Association (NASAA) – https://www.nasaa.org; 1-202-737-0900 (for obtaining the telephone number of the investor protection bureau of your state)

Financial Crimes Enforcement Network (FinCEN) – https://www.fincen.gov; Regulatory Helpline: 1-800-949-2732.

Select Documents:

Investment Advisers: What You Need to Know Before Choosing One, Securities and Exchange Commission, August 7, 2012.

(https://www.sec.gov/investor/pubs/invadvisers.htm)

Buying Prescription Medicine Online: A Consumer Safety Guide, Food and Drug Administration, October 14, 2012.

(https://www.fda.gov/drugs/resourcesforyou/ucm0805 88.htm)

Select Video:

An Age For Justice: Confronting Elder Abuse in America https://www.ncoa.org/public-policy-action/elder-justice/elder-justice-now/

REFERENCES

PREFACE

Kirchheimer, Sid. "Scams Trap Older Adults: 3 Reasons Why Older People Are More Prone to Cons." *AARP Bulletin Print Edition*, March 1, 2011.

Lawrence, D.H."Beautiful Old Age."
https://allpoetry.com/Beautiful-Old-Age

CHAPTER 1: Do the Right Thing

Acierno, Ron, Ph.D.; Melba Hernandez-Tejada, M.S.; Wendy Muzzy, B.S.; and Kenneth Steve M.S. "National Elder Mistreatment Study."
https://www.ncjrs.gov/pdffiles1/nij/grants/226456.pdf *Journal of Elder Abuse and Neglect*, Volume 25, Number 4, 2013, pages 281–293.

Administration on Aging. "Aging Statistics,"
https://aoa.acl.gov/Aging_Statistics/Index.aspx (last accessed on April 21, 2017).

Amour. Les Films du Losange,et al. 2012.

Archibald, John. "Alabama Closes Harper Lee Elder Abuse Investigation." *The Birmingham News*, March 12, 2015.

Balleisen, Edward J. *Fraud: An American History From Barnum to Madoff*. New Jersey: Princeton University Press, 2017.

Barron, James. "Brooke Astor's Son is Sentenced to Prison." *The New York Times*, December 21, 2009, page A31.

Berger, Marilyn. "Brooke Astor, 105, First Lady of Philanthropy, Dies." *The New York Times*, August 13, 2007.

Buettner, Russ. "Deemed Too Sick, Astor Son Is Paroled." *The New York Times*, August 22, 2013, page A21.

Fleeced: Speaking Out Against Senior Financial Abuse. National Community Reinvestment Coalition. 2013.

Fuchs, Erin. "The Heartbreaking Story of How Harper Lee Was Allegedly Robbed of the Copyright to Her Iconic Novel." *Business Insider*, February 3, 2015.

Grace, Melissa and Corkey Siemaszko. "Brooke Astor Grandson Philip Marshall, Anthony Marshall Son, Says Stepmom Charlene Deserves Jail." *New York Daily News*, October 9, 2009.

Legislature of Nebraska, One Hundred Fifth Legislature, First Session, Legislative Bill 122, Introduced by Pansing Brooks, January 6, 2017 (LB122, 2017).

Kovaleski, Serge F., Alexandra Alter, and Jennifer Crossley Howard. "Harper Lee's Condition Debated by Friends, Fans and Now State of Alabama." *The New York Times*, March 11, 2015.

National Council on Aging. (Statistics were provided by the National Council on Aging https://www.ncoa.org which is an organization that is designed to help those 60 and over meet the challenges of aging by provide community programs and services, online help, and advocacy in partnership with nonprofit organizations, government, and businesses.)

Nebraska. Paramount Pictures. 2013.

Pew Research Center. "Baby Boomers Retire." https://www.pewresearch.org/fact-tank/2010/12/29/baby-boomers-retire/ December 29, 2010. (The Pew Research

Center is a nonpartisan think tank that informs the public about the issues, attitudes and trends shaping America and the world. It conducts public opinion polling, demographic research, media content analysis and other empirical social science research. The Pew Research Center does not take policy positions. It is a subsidiary of The Pew Charitable Trusts.)

Rooney, Mickey. Testimony. Justice for All: Ending Elder Abuse, Neglect and Financial Exploitation, Senate Special Committee on Aging, March 2, 2011. (For a video of the full hearing: https://www.aging.senate.gov/hearings/justice-for-all-ending-elder-abuse-neglect-and-financial-exploitation and for a transcript of the full hearing: https://www.gpo.gov/fdsys/pkg/CHRG-112shrg66957/html/CHRG-112shrg66957.htm.) The United States Senate Special Committee on Aging was established in 1961 as a temporary committee, and it gained permanent status on February 1, 1977. As a special committee, it studies issues important to older Americans, like Medicare (including prescription drug pricing) and Social Security. Specifically, it can look into fraud and waste in these government programs. It also can issue public policy reports relating to the elderly, and can submit recommendations for legislation to the Senate. The Committee was reviewing health insurance coverage for older Americans prior to the enactment of the Social Security Amendments of 1965, which resulted in the creation of Medicare. Through the years, the Committee has brought to light unacceptable conditions in nursing homes, worked on adding more protections for the seniors in the area of age discrimination, and studied the Medicare system's incentives to hospitals to release patients "quicker and sicker." As America ages, the work of this Committee will only grow more critical. At the start of the 115th Congress (2017) the Committee was chaired by Senator Susan Collins (Republican-Maine) and its Ranking Member was Senator Bob Casey (Democrat-Pennsylvania).

Section 2011, Subtitle B – "Elder Justice." Social Security Act. (It defines "abuse" as "the knowing infliction of physical or psychological harm or the knowing deprivation of goods or services that are necessary to meet essential needs or to avoid physical or psychological harm." It defines the term "elder" as "an individual age 60 or older.")

Stevens, Laura and Jeffrey A. Trachtenberg. "Harper Lee Elder-Abuse Investigation Closed; Allegations 'Unfounded.'" *The Wall Street Journal*, April 3, 2015.

Stoddard, Martha. "In Lincoln, Daughters of Casey Kasem, Mickey Rooney Push Bill Aimed at Halting Isolation of Vulnerable Adults," *Omaha World-Herald*, February 17, 2017.

CHAPTER 2: The Signature Crime of the 21st Century

Blumenthal, Karen. "A Family's Fight to Save an Elder from Scammers: When the Patriarch Fell Prey to Thieves, Relatives Took Matters Into Their Own Hands," *The Wall Street Journal*, June 17, 2009.

Carter, Misty. "Elderly Fraud Scams: How Their Being Targeted and How to Prevent It." *Fraud Magazine*, January/February 2017.

Grace, Melissa and Corkey Siemaszko. "Brooke Astor Grandson Philip Marshall, Anthony Marshall Son, Says Stepmom Charlene Deserves Jail." *New York Daily News*, October 9, 2009.

Humphrey III, Hubert H. "Skip," Assistant Director of the Office for Older Americans - Consumer Financial Protection Bureau. Testimony. https://www.consumerfinance.gov/about-us/newsroom/testimony-of-hubert-h-skip-humphrey-iii-before-the-senate-subcommittee-on-financial-institutions-and-consumer-protection/ Senate Subcommittee on Financial Institutions and Consumer Protection, United States Senate Committee on Banking, Housing, and Urban Affairs Washington, D.C., November 15, 2011.

Kapadia, Reshma. "Financial Abuse: The Silent Epidemic." *Barron's*, November 12, 2016.

Knight, Victoria E. "Elder-Abuse Cases on the Rise." *The Wall Street Journal*, June 16, 2009.

MetLife. "The Metlife Study of Elder Financial Abuse: Crimes of Occasion, Desperation, and Predation Against America's Elders." https://www.metlife.com/assets/cao/mmi/publications/studies/2011/mmi-elder-financial-abuse.pdf, June 2011.

Smith, Asa Aarons. "Ask Asa: How to Find Your Missing Money," *WJCL News*, March 19, 2017.

Staff Reporter. "The Verdict in the Anthony Marshall Case." *New York Post*, October 8, 2009.

Staff Reporter. "Why You Shouldn't Give Your Doctor Your Social Security Number." *Consumer Reports*, February 10, 2015.

Stanford Center on Longevity and the FINRA Investor Education Foundation. "The State of Financial Fraud in America, Post-Conference Report." https://162.144.124.243/~longevl0/wp-content/uploads/2017/02/Fraud-Post-Conferece-Report-2-15-

17-2.pdf, November 30, 2016. (In 2011, Stanford University's Center on Longevity and the FINRA Investor Education Foundation launched the Financial Fraud Research Center, which is a resource for law enforcement, the government and research groups studying how Americans lose billions of dollars each year to fraud.)

True Link. "The True Link Report on Elder Financial Abuse 2015," https://truelink-wordpress-assets.s3.amazonaws.com/wp-content/uploads/True-Link-Report-On-Elder-Financial-Abuse-012815.pdf, 2015.

Tzu, Sun. *The Art of War*, Translated by Thomas Cleary. Boston: Shambala Publications, Inc., 1988. (While the quote is from https://www.goodreads.com/quotes/720920-every-battle-is-won-before-it-s-ever-fought, one of the commentaries in the work states, more precisely, "…you have won before you have even done battle…".)

Warren, Lydia and Associated Press, "Brooke Astor's Son Tony Marshall - Who Was Locked Up For Looting Her $200 Million Estate - Dies Aged 90," *DailyMail,* December 1, 2014.

CHAPTER 3: A Losing Bet For Seniors and a Jackpot For Scammers

Balleisen, Edward J. *Fraud: An American History From Barnum to Madoff.* New Jersey: Princeton University Press, 2017.

Blumenthal, Karen. "How Banks, Marketers Aid Scams," *The Wall Street Journal*, July 15, 2009.

Crary, David."Losses Mount From Scams Targeting Older Americans." *Associated Press*, March 3, 2012.

Federal Trade Commission. Consumer Sentinel Network Data Book (formerly, Consumer Sentinel Annual Fraud and

Identity Theft Reports), 2002-2015. ("Prizes/Sweepstakes and Lotteries" are "Promotions for "free" prizes for a fee; foreign lotteries and sweepstakes offered through the phone, fax, e-mail or mail, etc.".)

Glor, Jeff. "Inside the 'Jamaican Lottery Scam': How U.S. Seniors Become Targets." *CBS This Morning*, March 12, 2013.

Huffman, Mark. "Magic Jack Being Used in Phone Spoofing Scam: Scam Shows Up in Mississippi." *ConsumerAffairs.com*, November 29, 2011.

Kroft, Steve. "The So-Called Canadian Lottery Scam." *60 Minutes*, September 26, 2004.

Leung, Rebecca. "Lottery Scam Targets Elderly." *60 Minutes*, February 11, 2009.

Ritchie, Rochelle. "Foreign Lottery Scam Costs 81-Year-Old Nearly Half A Million Dollars." *CBS Baltimore*, March 7, 2013.

Tao, Dominick. "New Take on Old SCAM; A Type of Nigerian Scam Out of Canada Offers $150,000 to a Retired Railroad Engineer in Dunedin." *The St. Petersburg Times*, December 3, 2009

U.S. Postal Service. "Don't Get Scammed, Get the Facts!" https://www.deliveringtrust.com/ (This website of the U.S. Postal Service discusses International Lottery Fraud.)

CHAPTER 4: Giving With Your Heart and Head

Charities Aid Foundation. World Giving Index 2011, A Global View of Giving Trends, 2011.

Charity Navigator. "Evaluating Charities Not Currently Rated by Charity Navigator."

https://www.charitynavigator.org/index.cfm?bay=content.view&cpid=847 (last accessed on March 28, 2017).

_____. "Questions to Ask Charities Before Donating: Tips For How to Investigate a Charity's Results." https://www.charitynavigator.org/index.cfm?bay=content.view&cpid=1209 (last accessed on March 28, 2017).

_____. "Top 10 Best Practices of Savvy Donors." https://www.charitynavigator.org/index.cfm?bay=content.view&cpid=4756 (last accessed on March 28, 2017).

_____. "What to Do When a Charity Calls." https://www.charitynavigator.org/index.cfm?bay=content.view&cpid=224 (last accessed on March 28, 2017).

Federal Trade Commission. "FTC Warns Consumers: Charity Scams Often Follow Disasters." https://www.ftc.gov/news-events/press-releases/2013/05/ftc-warns-consumers-charity-scams-often-follow-disasters, May 24, 2013.

New York State Office of the Attorney General. https://www.charitiesnys.com/RegistrySearch/search_charities.jsp (last accessed on February 17, 2017).

Silverman, Rachel Emma and Sally Beatty. "Doing Due Diligence on Your Donations." *The Wall Street Journal*, December 20. 2007.

Smith, Aaron. "Americans Donated a Record $373 Billion to Charity in 2015." *CNNMoney*, June 14, 2016.

Staff Reporter. "A.G. Schneiderman Obtains Court Decision Ordering Major Long Island Fundraiser to Pay $3.1 Million in Restitution for Defrauding Donors." *Targeted News Service*, June 13, 2013.

_____. "Brooklyn Couple Accused Of Using Ailing 5-Year-Old Boy's Photo For Charity Scam Arrested." *CBS New York*, March 4, 2017.

_____. "Don't Be Taken in by Charity Scams." *Consumer Reports* News, July 19, 2013.

_____. "New York: A.G. Schneiderman Launches Review of Breast Cancer Consumer Campaigns." *U.S. Official News*, October 28, 2011.

_____. "Rebecca Riccio Receives National Attention for Giving With Purpose Course." *Associated Press*, July 14, 2013.

_____. "Where Are Your Charity Dollars Going?" *CNBC*, December 9, 2010.

_____. "Woman Accused of Sandy Hook Fraud Sentenced to 8 Months in Prison With 2 Years' Probation." *NBC Connecticut*, October 12, 2013.

Tozzi, John. "Online Extra: Charity Begins with Due Diligence." *BloombergBusinessweek*, November 25, 2007.

US Supreme Court. Illinois ex rel. Madigan v. Telemarketing Associates, Inc., Et. Al., 538 U.S. 600, 2003.

Woodruff, Judy. "In Arizona, Out of Control Wildfire Kills 19 Members of Elite Firefighting Team." *PBS Newshour*, July 1, 2013.

Yan, Holly, Eliott C. McLaughlin, and Jason Hanna, "Loss of 19 Firefighters in Arizona Blaze 'Unbearable,' Governor Says." *CNN*, July 2, 2013.

CHAPTER 5: Don't Take The Bait!

Greenberg, Pam. "Zombies, Trojan Horses and You." *State Legislatures*, May 2011.

Holtfreter, Robert E., Ph.D., CFE, CICA. "Facebook Phishing Schemes Are Turning 'Friends' Into Enemies." *Fraud Magazine*, July/August 2013.

Merz, Theo. "Academics Launch 'Phishing' Block." *The Telegraph*, August 21, 2013.

National Security Agency. "Best Practices for Keeping Your Home Network Secure." https://dodcio.defense.gov/Portals/0/Documents/Cyber/Slick sheet_BestPracticesForKeepingYourHomeNetworkSecure_Web _update.pdf, May 2014.

Staff Reporter. "'Phishing' and Other Online Identity Theft Scams: Don't Take the Bait." *Save and Invest*, February 29, 2012.

Staff Reporter. "Phishing Kits – The Same Wolf, Just a Different Sheep's Clothing." *RSA Monthly Online Fraud Report*, February 2013.

CHAPTER 6: Like Kin, But Less Than Kind

Balleisen, Edward J. *Fraud: An American History From Barnum to Madoff*. New Jersey: Princeton University Press, 2017.

Marquet, Christopher T. "The Marquet Report on Ponzi Schemes: A White-Collar Fraud Study of Major Ponzi-Type Investment Fraud Cases Revealed From 2002-2011." *Marquet International*, June 2, 2011.

Marquet, Christopher T. "12 Steps to Avoid Ponzi Schemes & Investment Frauds." *Marquet International*, May 28,

2011.

National Futures Association. "Scams and Swindles: An Educational Guide to Avoiding Investment Fraud." https://www.nfa.futures.org/nfa-investor-information/publication-library/scams-and-swindles.pdf, 2007.

North American Securities Administrators Association. "Affinity Fraud: Beware of Swindlers Who Claim Loyalty to Your Group." https://www.nasaa.org/7157/affinity-fraud-beware-of-swindlers-who-claim-loyalty-to-your-group/ (last accessed on March 28, 2017).

Sargsian, Karina. "A Wolf in Sheep's Clothing: Enacting Statutes Enhancing Criminal Penalties for Affinity Fraud." *Social Science Research Network*, February 16, 2012.

SEC Office of Investor Education and Advocacy. "A Guide For Seniors: Protect Yourself Against Investment Fraud." https://www.sec.gov/investor/seniors/seniorsguide.pdf, May 2013.

SEC Office of Investor Education and Advocacy. "Stopping Affinity Fraud in Your Community: How to Avoid Investment Scams that Target Groups." https://www.sec.gov/investor/pubs/affinity.pdf, April 2009.

Securities and Exchange Commission. "SEC Charges Pastor With Defrauding Retirees." https://www.sec.gov/news/press-release/2017-74#, March 30, 2017.

CHAPTER 7: RoboCop For Robocallers?

Federal Communications Commission. Robocall Strike Force Report. https://transition.fcc.gov/cgb/Robocall-Strike-Force-Final-Report.pdf (last accessed on March 28, 2017).

Federal Communications Commission. "Advanced Methods to Target and Eliminate Unlawful Robocalls." https://transition.fcc.gov/Daily_Releases/Daily_Business/2017/db0302/DOC-343731A1.pdf (last accessed on March 28, 2017).

Feran, Tim. "On the Do Not Call List But Still Getting Calls? Here's Why." *The Columbus Dispatch*, March 14, 2017.

RoboCop. Orion Pictures. 1987.

CHAPTER 8: Investigate Before You Invest

Gordon, Marcy. "3 Charged in Voicemail Stock Scheme." *Fox News*, July 28, 2006.

OTCMarkets. "The Markets." https://www.otcmarkets.com/marketplaces/otc-pink (accessed on March 28, 2017).

OTC Markets, "OTC Markets Group's Policy Regarding Caveat Emptor," https://www.otcmarkets.com/learn/caveat-emptor (last accessed on March 28, 2017).

Securities and Exchange Commission. "SEC Charges Florida Promoters and the Voice Behind Fraudulent 'Wrong Number' Stock Tips." https://www.sec.gov/news/press/2006/2006-124.htm, July 27, 2006.

Securities and Exchange Commission. "'Wrong Numbers' and Stock Tips on Your Answering Machine." https://www.sec.gov/reportspubs/investor-publications/investorpubswrongnumberscamhtm.html, January 27, 2006.

The Graduate. Lawrence Turman.1967. (The start of the quote "I just want to say one word to you. Just one word. Are you listening?" is from this movie, and the character ends the quote with "Plastics," not "Lithium.")

CHAPTER 9: Robbing Peter To Pay Paul

Agar, John. "Woman, 70, Sent to Prison in 'Jaw-Dropping' $7.5M Ponzi Scheme." *The Ann Arbor News*, February 22, 2017.

Browning, Lynnley. "Breathless Pitches For Penny Stocks, Now in Newspapers." *The New York Times,* September 5, 2007.

Fanelli, James. "Lawyer Claims He Was Conned in Ponzi Scheme By Guy He Met in Criminal Court," *dnainfo*, February 23, 2017.

Levy, Steven. "My Secret Life as a Penny-Stock Tout." *Newsweek*, July 24, 2006.

McCoy, Kevin. "Ex-Sleepy's Exec Says He Was Lured Into Alleged 'Hamilton' Ponzi Scheme." *USA Today*, February 8, 2017.

Montagne, Renee. "Penny Stock Scams Still Cheating Millions." *NPR Morning Edition*, June 15, 2007.

Pulham, Mark. "The Great Ponzi." *Crime Magazine*, August 6, 2012.

Russell, Francis. "Bubble, Bubble – No Toil, No Trouble." *Stories of Great Crimes & Trials*. New York: American Heritage, pages 235-242.

Scott, David Clark. "Heirs of Original Ponzi Scheme Can Still Fleece the Unwary, *Christian Science Monitor*, March 24, 1986.

SEC Office of Investor Education and Advocacy. "Investor Alert: Social Media and Investing – Avoiding Fraud." https://www.sec.gov/investor/alerts/socialmediaandfraud.pdf, January 2012.

Securities and Exchange Commission. "Ten Questions About Any Investment Opportunity." https://www.sec.gov/investor/pubs/cyberfraud/questions, February 25, 1999.

_____. "Tips for Checking Out Newsletters." https://www.sec.gov/investor/pubs/cyberfraud/newsletter.htm , February 27, 2009.

_____. "How To Avoid Fraud," https://www.sec.gov/reportspubs/investorpublications/investo rpubsavoidfraudhtm.html, June 9, 2009.

Seyd, Jane. "West Vancouver Woman Admits to $30M Ponzi Scheme," *North Shore News*, April 20, 2017.

Staff Reporter. "Citron Reports on Lithium Exploration (OTCBB: LEXG) – A Nostalgic Piece For the 'Old Lemon,'" *Citron Research*, April 28, 2011.

_____. "Massachusetts-Based Penny Stock Promoter Orders to Pay Over $1.6M in Penny Stock Fraud Case." *US Fed News Service*, July 27, 2013.

_____. "SEC Charges San Diego-Based Promoter in Penny Stock Scheme," *US Fed News Service*, June 22, 2013.

Tex, Ethan. "Who Was Ponzi & What Was His Scheme?" *Mental Floss*, December 16, 2008.

Tierney, Karen J. "FRAUDBASICS: Con Schemes Abound, Part One." *Fraud Magazine*, January/February 2003.

Universal Postal Union. "About international reply coupons." https://www.upu.int/nc/en/activities/international-reply-coupons/about-irc.html (accessed on March 28, 2017).

Wells, Joseph T., CFE, CPA. "How Ponzi Prospered: Famous Scheme Produced Millions Before Pyramid Collapsed." *Fraud Magazine*, March/April 2001.

Zuckoff, Mitchell. *Ponzi's Scheme: The True Story of a Financial Legend.* New York: Random House Trade, 2005. (According to Zuckoff, one explanation for the phrase robbing Peter to pay Paul "traces it to the 1500s in England, when the lands of St. Peter's Church at Westminster were sold to fund repairs at St. Paul's Cathedral in London." Page 104.)

CHAPTER 10: Wooed By a Website

Ajamie, Tom and Bruce Kelly. *Financial Serial Killers: Inside the World of Wall Street Money Hustlers, Swindlers, and Con Men.* New York: Skyhorse Publishing, 2014.

Cole, Benjamin Mark. "Barry Minkow's Treatment in Press Exposes Reporters' Own Vulnerability to Fraud." *Los Angeles Business Journal,* July 13, 187, page 10.

Mr. Deeds Goes to Town. Columbia Pictures Corporation. 1936.

North American Securities Administrators Association. "Top Investor Threats." https://www.nasaa.org/3752/top-investor-threats/ (accessed on March 28, 2017).

Securities and Exchange Commission. "'Guaranteed' High Returns. https://www.sec.gov/rss/your_money/guaranteed_high_returns.htm (accessed on March 28, 2017).

CHAPTER 11: Fraud Is Infinite In Variety

Ligaya, Armina. "Counterfeit Drugs Cause Woman's Death, Coroner Concludes." *The Globe and Mail*, July 6, 2007.

Reddaway v. Banham (1896) A.C. 199, 221.

CHAPTER 12: By Jove, You Were Right!

(There are no references for this chapter.)

CHAPTER 13: Like Taking Candy From a Baby

(There are no references for this chapter.)

CHAPTER 14: Fade to Black

Department of Justice. "Thirteen Charged in Miami Lakes and California Boiler Rooms Securities Fraud Scheme that Defrauded Over 700 Investors." https://www.justice.gov/usao-sdfl/pr/thirteen-charged-miami-lakes-and-california-boiler-rooms-securities-fraud-scheme, September 26, 2016.

Ropes & Gray. "The SEC Speaks 2017: Division of Enforcement Highlights." https://www.ropesgray.com/newsroom/alerts/2017/03/The-SEC-Speaks-2017-Division-of-Enforcement-Highlights.aspx, March 10, 2017.

Securities and Exchange Commission. "SEC Charges CEO and Boiler Room Operator With Fraud." *Litigation Release No. 23658*, September 28, 2016.

CHAPTER 15: Criminal Minds

Alighieri, Dante. *The Divine Comedy*. Christian Classics Ethereal Library, 2017.

Boiler Room. New Line Cinema. 2000.

Cialdini, Robert B., PhD. *Influence: The Psychology of Persuasion*. New York: William Morrow, 1993.

Cialdini, Robert, PhD. *Pre-Suasion: A Revolutionary Way to Influence and Persuade*. New York: Simon & Schuster, 2016.

Financial Industry Regulatory Authority. "FINRA Bars Broker for Converting and Improperly Using More Than $500,000 from a Catholic Nun's Holdings, Another $80,000 from Three Elderly Customers," May 5, 2009.

Kroft, Steve. "The So-Called Canadian Lottery Scam." *60 Minutes*, September 26, 2004.

McMenamin, Brigid. "The Banker and the Nun." *Forbes*, October 10, 1997.

Pratkanis, Anthony and Doug Shadel. *Weapons of Fraud: A Source Book For Fraud Fighters*, AARP Washington, 2005.

Shadel, Douglas P. and John T., *Schemes & Scams: A Practical Guide for Outwitting Today's Con Artist For the 50+ Generation*. California: Newcastle Publishing, 1994.

The Third Man. London Film Productions. 1949.

CHAPTER 16: Know Thyself

Cohen, Gabriel. "For You, Half Price." *The New York Times*, November 27, 2005.

Confidence Girl. Andrew L. Stone Productions. 1952.

Rosefsky, Robert S. *Frauds, Swindles, and Rackets: A Red Alert for Today's Consumers*. Chicago: Follett Publishing Company, 1973.

CHAPTER 17: A Fraud Fighter's Tools of the Trade

Clifton, Brian, Sam Lavigne, and Francis Tseng. "Predicting Financial Crime: Augmenting the Predictive Policing Arsenal." *The New Inquiry*, April 26, 2017.

Gillers, Heather. "What You Won't Learn From One Wall Street Watchdog." *The Wall Street Journal*, March 21, 2017.

Shadel, Douglas P. and John T. *Schemes & Scams: A Practical Guide for Outwitting Today's Con Artist For the 50+ Generation*. California: Newcastle Publishing, 1994.

Sutherland, Edwin H. "White Collar Criminality." *American Sociological Review*, Volume 5, Number 1, February 1940.

CHAPTER 18: Recommendations

Balleisen, Edward J. *Fraud: An American History From Barnum to Madoff*. New Jersey: Princeton University Press, 2017.

Bengali, Shashank. "Inside the Indian IRS Scam That Cheated US Taxpayers Out of Millions." *Los Angeles Times*, November 22, 2016.

Consumer Financial Protection Bureau, "Advisory for Financial Institutions on Preventing and Responding to Elder Financial Exploitation," https://files.consumerfinance.gov/f/201603_cfpb_advisory-for-financial-institutions-on-preventing-and-responding-to-elder-financial-exploitation.pdf, March 2016.

Consumer Financial Protection Bureau, "Recommendations and Report for Financial Institutions on Preventing and Responding to Elder Financial Exploitation," https://files.consumerfinance.gov/f/201603_cfpb_recommendations-and-report-for-financial-institutions-on-preventing-and-responding-to-elder-financial-exploitation.pdf, March 2016.

Council For Economic Education. Survey of the States: Economic and Personal Finance Education in Our Nation's Schools, 2016. (According to the survey, "[e]very two years, the Council for Economic Education (CEE) comprehensively reviews the state of K-12 economic and financial education in the United States, collecting data from all 50 states and the District of Columbia. The biennial Survey of the States serves as an important benchmark for our progress, revealing both how far we've come and how far we still have to go. There has been notable progress since the first survey was published in 1998, yet the pace of change has slowed.")

Financial Crimes Enforcement Network, "Advisory to Financial Institutions on Filing Suspicious Activity Reports Regarding Elder Financial Exploitation," https://www.fincen.gov/statutes_regs/guidance/html/fin-2011-a003.html, February 22, 2011.

Financial Crimes Enforcement Network, *The SAR Activity Review: Trends, Tips, and Issues (Issue 23)*, May 2013.

Financial Industry Regulatory Authority. "FINRA Receives SEC Approval on Rule Proposal Addressing Financial Exploitation of Seniors." http://www.finra.org/newsroom/2017/finra-receives-sec-approval-rule-proposal-addressing-financial-exploitation-seniors, March 30, 2017.

_____. "FINRA Senior Helpline Marks Second Anniversary With $4.3 Million in Voluntary Reimbursements to Callers," April 20, 2017.

Venkataraman, Ayesha. "Indian Man Accused in Multimillion-Dollar Call-Center Swindle Is Held." *The New York Times*, April 8, 2017.

ABOUT THE AUTHOR

John Rotondi has worked in the financial services industry for over 20 years, as both a regulator and compliance officer. In addition, he has previously served as a volunteer with the Fixed Income Analysts Society, Inc. (FIASI), where he was Treasurer; the Foreign Services Volunteer Corps (FSVC), making presentations concerning compliance, risk management, and stock market structure to Russian regulatory authorities; and he was selected by the U.S. Treasury Secretary to serve on the Citizen Advocacy Panel (CAP), which listens to taxpayers, identifies taxpayers' issues, and make suggestions for improving IRS service and customer satisfaction. John is a Certified Public Accountant (CPA), Certified Fraud Examiner (CFE), Certified Anti- Money Laundering Specialist (CAMS), and Certified Regulatory and Compliance Professional (CRCP). John earned a BS in Finance and an MBA from St. John's University. You may contact him at johnrotondi8@gmail.com

www.ingramcontent.com/pod-product-compliance
Lightning Source LLC
Chambersburg PA
CBHW072124280526
45788CB00002B/530